THE CONSCIOUS MIND

THE CONSCIOUS MIND
A Developmental Theory

A.J. Malerstein, M.D.

 HUMAN SCIENCES PRESS, INC.
72 FIFTH AVENUE
NEW YORK, N.Y. 10011

Printed in the United States of America
123456789   987654321

Library of Congress Cataloging-in-Publication Data

Malerstein, A. J. (Abraham J.)
   The conscious mind.

   Bibliography: p. 153.
   Includes index.
   1. Consciousness—Physiological aspects.
2. Psychology, Physiological. 3. Developmental
psychobiology. I. Title. [DNLM: 1. Consciousness—
physiology. 2. Psychophysiology. WL 705 M245c]
QP411.M35   1986   153   85-21893
ISBN 0-89885-273-0

CONTENTS

PREFACE

It is not surprising that I failed in my initial attempts to read Piaget's works, since with some exceptions Piaget's writings make difficult reading. After each attempt I comforted myself with the rationalization, "Anyone who is that difficult to understand must have little to say." Later, Mary Ahern suggested that I read Piaget as part of a literature review for a book we were writing. Easy for her to say! Fortunately, I read Maier's (1965) book in which he compared Erikson's, Piaget's, and Sears's work. In addition to finding Maier easy to understand, I became intrigued by a type of reasoning he described. This type of reasoning was observed by Piaget in two- to four-year-olds. Those children's thought processes corresponded to thought processes I had observed in a group of adults whom I later called symbolic characters. Then began the difficult, but rewarding, excursion through many of Piaget's works. This was followed by a major reorganization of our book on character structure (Malerstein and Ahern, 1982).

In the course of reading Piaget's works, particularly his studies of his own children, I sensed that they contained a theory of consciousness. The theory was elusive. At times, I thought I had a grasp of the concepts involved. At other times, I lost it. Finally, after the book on character structure was published, I went through Piaget's writings in search of the theory. This book is the result of that search. In the course of my search I realized that this theory, implicit in his findings, was not one intended by Piaget. This implicit theory and much of Piaget's other work fit recent organic findings, understandings of certain clinical syndromes, as well as computer function.

Three major issues are addressed in this book: (1) how the essence of consciousness is constructed as waking state schemes; (2) how brain function underlies psychological function; and (3) how to bring together Piaget's cognitive-developmental system with psychodynamic clinical understandings largely derived from Freud's work.

Adapting one of Freud's hypotheses I explain consciousness as a differentiation of thought and perception from more primitive configurations. In the course of developing this thesis, a bridge between the organic and the psychological is proposed. All along Piaget's concepts and Freud's are compared and contrasted to show in some measure how Piaget's structural/constructionist conceptualizations fit current dynamic clinical understandings, most of which grew out of Freud's concepts and findings. Integration of dynamic psychiatry with Piaget's cognitive-developmental system provides theoretical underpinnings for a general psychology, especially once affect, the third major conscious form, is integrated into the system.

In Chapter 1, similarities and differences of Freud's energic psychology and Piaget's structuralist psychology are discussed. Chapter 2 and the latter part of Chapter 1 provide a Piagetian frame of reference and an abbreviated review of Piaget's stages of cognitive development, especially the sensorimotor period, in preparation for Chapter 3. In Chapter 3, basing my concepts, in part, on recent understandings of neuro-physiology of the visual system of the brain, I show how myelination of the tract leading to the primary visual area of the brain could induce the reorganization of cognition which then enables the child to construct visual objects that are distinct from one another. These concepts constitute a model for understanding the interaction of psychologic development with brain development.

Chapters 4, 5 and 6 address consciousness. Piaget's findings and theories regarding consciousness are reviewed in Chapter 4, including his proposal that awareness progresses from knowledge of one's intended goal and of the result to knowledge of how one acts and how the object acts. In Chapters 5 and 6 I take issue with Piaget's thesis that consciousness is an emergent construct, a product of restructuring at different stages of development. I suggest that consciousness is present at the outset as the waking state, a state of connectedness between the central and peripheral nervous systems. Further, I show that Piaget's stages of sensorimotor cognitive development trace the forms taken by consciousness until percept and mental image are differentiated from each other.

In Chapter 7, affect, the component of consciousness, distinct from percept and mental image or thought, is addressed. Once again Piaget's concepts and Freud's are compared including the difference a structural versus an energic theory of the psyche makes to conceptualization and treatment of patients. Recent findings and theories regarding the biology of affect, including drug treatment of mood disorders, are incorporated into a view of the origins and function of affect in the psychobiology of the individual.

This amalgam of biologic findings with dynamic clinical psychiatry and cognitive-developmental psychology addresses the affective, cognitive, and perceptual, the pathologic and non-pathologic, and the conscious and un-conscious.

Finally, in Chapter 8 certain implications of this theoretical model are drawn: where memory is located, why a structural system that reorganizes itself is more stable than an energic one, and how this structural theory modifies one's treatment approach.

I wish to thank Cynthia Hall for her editorial assistance and C.P. for her preparation of the manuscript.

Chapter 1

INTRODUCTION

Piaget's work provides us with basic tools for bridging the gap between thought and brain function and for explaining consciousness. This book outlines how maturation of a unit of the central nervous system may serve cognitive development as well as how Piaget's findings and some of his concepts can be adapted to demystify consciousness. The present work is a slight detour from our efforts to synthesize clinical findings with Piaget's cognitive-developmental system (Malerstein & Ahern, 1982).

Piaget and Freud

Piaget believed that there was a natural alliance between his work and Freud's. In 1922 he presented a paper at the Psychoanalytic Congress in Berlin in which he pointed out some parallels between toddlers' thinking and unconscious or psychotic thought processes (Piaget, 1962a). He wrote that his paper drew some interest. The concepts presented there, however, did not become a part of the psychoanalytic body of knowledge, although recently several psychiatrists have drawn attention to this parallel between the thought processes of two- to four-year-olds[1] and those of schizophrenics.[2]

Later Piaget (1962a) called for an overhaul of psychoanalytic theory and translated certain psychoanalytic discoveries into his own theoretical constructs. While there have been amendments to psychoanalytic theory, the total overhaul that Piaget thought necessary does not appear likely to occur from within the ranks of the psychoanalysts, although many psychoanalysts are discontent with small or large segments of psychoanalytic theory. From time to time some remodeling seems to take place (Hartmann, Kris, & Lowenstein, 1964; Rapaport, 1967; Kohut, 1977). Since Freud, however, there has been no leader of the psychoanalytic movement. As a body, psychoanalysts are at once too fragmented and too vested to permit a major reworking. No single voice has sufficient influence, and certainly the task is not the kind that a committee could do.

Piaget's position on the synthesis of his work with Freud's is perhaps best illustrated in his address to the American Psychoanalytic Association. "I am convinced that there will be a time when the psychology of cognitive functions and psychoanalysis will have to blend into a general theory which will improve both by correcting each, and it is this future that is worth preparing by showing presently the relations which can exist between them" (Piaget, 1973, p. 31). In his presentation Piaget documented examples of repression in the cognitive domain. Such findings permit a more general theory of repression than Freud's, since, as will be shown, Piaget's theory embraces both the cognitive and affective domains.

Piaget's Theory

Piaget insisted that there was no Piagetian system. This stance was in keeping with his wish that his work not be made the nidus for the formation of a cult, as Freud's work became. Piaget wanted his work to be assimilated into the general stream of science. The sincerity of this wish was evident at the 1976 meeting of the Jean Piaget Society in Philadelphia. Several thousand social scientists attended, many of whom would have eagerly rallied around Piaget as a kind of living monument. The level of adulation in this audience could easily have been mobilized into a movement. But the principal speakers each made the point that Piaget's wish was to inspire people to do their own work, and that his hope was that some of his work would be incorporated into the general body of science. This attitude was exemplified by Piaget's presenting a bit of his latest work, rather than using the podium to summarize his work or his position or to give an inspirational lecture.

In spite of Piaget's contention that he had no system, in the sense of a preconceived framework or thesis, a number of factors suggest that he did or that he discovered one. He was painstakingly precise in delineating his concepts and how they differed from those of other investigators. His terminology, including schemes,[3] assimilation, and accommodation; his guiding principles—stressing constructivism, interactionism, and holism; his stage theory of development; and even, to some extent, his methodology, all combine to demarcate a system. Perhaps his efforts at consistency, his demand for empirical validity, and his unparalleled observational acuity, coupled with his broad-based knowledge of science, especially the biological sciences including embryology, and his remarkable ability to conceptualize at the most general level in any theory-

building, all combined to approximate the true psychologic process such that they naturally form a system. In
any case, there is much in Piaget's work and his concepts
that distinguishes them from any other partial or whole
psychologic system. No other psychologic body of knowledge has the inner coherence of Piaget's, always remaining
consistent with the two basic biological models, that of digestive function and that of epigenetic embryologic development.

Piaget's theory is primarily structuralist. According to
his theory, transformation of cognitive structures parallels
embryologic restructuring, with primitive, global structures reorganizing in stages into more differentiated structures. Digestive mechanisms, assimilation and accommodation, operate at the open boundaries of the structures.
Like other biological structures, cognitive structure is open
to interaction with the surround, but is not merely respondent to it.

Freud's theory, in contrast, is basically an energic one.
His system is analogous to the power systems of nineteenth
century physics. His system is fluid, with energy trans-
forming itself into structure, e.g., the ego and superego.

Piaget's and Freud's methodologies were similar. Both
Piaget and Freud relied primarily on careful observations
of small groups of subjects, sometimes just one or two
cases. With children who were old enough to be verbal
Piaget used what he termed the clinical method, not
greatly different from an unstructured psychotherapeutic
interview in which the interviewer follows the subject's
lead, employing the subject's terminology, but asking clari-
fying questions as they explore the child's understanding
of a particular phenomenon. Since Piaget's objectives were
investigative (not therapeutic) he might, in the end, chal-
lenge the child to some extent in order either to press for
the limits of the child's understanding or to test the child's
degree of conviction regarding his own answers. This chal-

lenging is not, of course, a part of the unstructured psychotherapeutic interview of psychoanalysis.

Piaget's Observations

While both the psychoanalysts and Piaget have been
criticized for the small size of their series and their failure
to use control subjects, it is difficult to imagine a more rigorous scientific investigation than Freud's (1953a) study of
the obsessive personality or Deutsch's (1942) discovery of
the borderline which she called the "as-if" personality.
Similarly, Piaget's numerous painstaking observations and
his meticulously varying the conditions of his observations
in order to ferret out the level of the child's understanding
is perhaps unparalleled in scientific investigations, even
though some of his best work was confined to the study of
his own three children: Piaget, *The Construction of Reality in
the Child*, 1954; *The Origins of Intelligence in Children*, 1963;
and *Play, Dreams and Imitation in Childhood*, 1962a. Piaget
regularly used simple experimental situations; for example, how an infant dealt with a bottle that was handed
to him with the nipple facing away (Piaget, 1954) or how
a five-year-old grouped objects whose attributes such as
shape or color differed (Inhelder & Piaget, 1969). Then
he varied the situation, observed the child a day or a
month later, and, if the child was old enough, probed him
with questions and followed his lead in posing follow-up
questions. From such investigations Piaget was able to infer the child's constructs, the level of coordination of his
schemes.
    One of the many examples contained in the three
books involves the child's use of a stick (Piaget, 1963).
Piaget's two daughters at around eighteen months of age
learned, in steps, to use a stick as an instrument to obtain
an object that was out of reach. He described each phase of
their piecemeal learning, referring to it as an acquisition

through apprenticeship. Piaget's son had not been exposed to learning to use a stick as a tool, although he already had the ability to construct mental representations of objects. When presented with a problem that could be solved by use of a stick as a tool, he skipped the apprenticeship. He not only immediately used the stick as an instrument, but readily substituted one sticklike object for another. Piaget then concluded that once a child has the ability to represent, he has a whole new system for cognizing a system that may supersede the less mature one. This inference, based on observation of a single child compared to only two other children, became one piece of support in understanding development in stages that involve reorganizations of structures.

The Two Giants

Freud held to his concepts tenaciously: that of psychic energy and determinism was never forsaken. Though such formulations eventually limited his theory, they were the faith and the base from which he was able to create a science of the unconscious and a treatment system. Illustrative of his tenacity and creative genius were his discovery and elucidation of transference reactions in psychoanalysis. Freud discovered that these intense reactions originated in (were transferred from) components of past relationships which are reenacted rather than recalled in the psychoanalytic situation. When faced with these intense feelings of the patient, Freud's colleague, Breuer, dropped the method of treatment while Freud, committed to determinism, formulated his concept of transference. He refused to view these feelings as mere perturbations in the system, but saw them as explainable, determined by earlier experiences (or fantasies). Transference phenomena supported the concept of an unconscious and became the cornerstone of psychoanalysis as a treatment. Freud's elucidation of dreams, symptoms, slips of the tongue, and free associations, all consonant with an assumption of (psychic) determinism, further supported the notion that we have an unconscious system which uses a different logic than our adult conscious logic.

If in Piaget's work there is a faith and base comparable to Freud's in psychic energy and determinism, it might be that psychic function and structure are isomorphic with biologic function and structure; and that an explanation of adult phenomena must rest upon tracing the epigenesis of such phenomena.

Freud and Piaget are the two twentieth-century giants in the field of psychology. While there are omissions and errors in the contributions of both, many of Freud's clinical findings will probably endure, and the gross outlines of Piaget's theory and most of his findings probably will survive. Though perhaps Piaget could not have made his discoveries if Freud had not made his, Piaget's work may eventually prove of greater moment.

Piaget's Schemes

Freud and the psychoanalysts and the psychotherapists who followed him spent the greater part of their professional lives tracing the vicissitudes of unconscious cognition. As a result of this effort much is known about the variety and richness of normal and abnormal thoughts and behavior that are manipulated unconsciously. The styles of manipulation may be subsumed under the three basic ones, condensation, displacement, and representation by opposites, plus the defense mechanisms, e.g., denial, conversion, isolation, and reaction formation. All these mechanisms may be viewed as relationships between Piaget's schemes. Initially they are types of failure to differentiate between schemes. Later they are coordinations which are invoked to manipulate schemes actively, serving equilibration between different schemes (in psychoanalytic terms, serving conflict).

Piaget's *scheme,* his basic building block of the psyche, is a hypothetical, organized, holistic unit of the psyche which is analogous to a biological cell or organ. Piaget traced the reorganizations of schemes, beginning with primitive reflex schemes such as sucking and grasping, and culminating in adolescence with formal operational thought. The sucking scheme, corresponding initially to the infant's built-in sucking reflex, is the clustering of all the motor and sensory system activities that are involved in sucking. Not only is the sucking scheme the entirety of central nervous system activity related to the sensorimotor activity of sucking, but also it includes any other frequently related co-temporaneous activity, e.g., the feel of a bottle, the warmth from another body, sensations from the surround. It includes at least the entire pattern of sensory stimulation of touch, taste, state of satiation, warmth, proprioception from the mouth, jaw, tongue, etc., and any feedback within the brain of the motor impulses that direct sucking behavior. The proprioceptive activity resulting from movement of the mouth, head, and neck during sucking are as much a part of the sucking scheme as taste or touch.

In parallel fashion proprioceptive and motor activity serving the head, neck, and eye muscles are as much a part of a visual scheme as is retinal stimulation. This is one reason that Piaget refers to the child's watching an object as acting on it with his eyes. The other reason for use of "acting upon" with the eyes instead of simply seeing is to emphasize the tendency of a scheme to *assimilate,* actively and selectively, patterns of sensorimotor stimulation that have a configurational resemblance to it.

Like any other biologic structure, a scheme requires *nutrient* or *aliment* to sustain itself. For the sucking scheme the aliment is all sensorimotor activity related to sucking:

contact with the breast, warmth, position, and all other at-
tendant relationships. While a scheme requires aliment for
sustenance, it does not become the aliment any more than
an animal becomes a cabbage by eating cabbage. Nevertheless, it *accommodates* to nuances in the aliment that it assimilates and thereby is modified. Evidence of this accommodation is the child's shaping his mouth differently when
sucking a finger than when sucking a nipple, or his becoming more skilled at sucking either a finger or a nipple. The
sucking scheme will accommodate to patterns of sensorimotor activity arising from sucking a finger or a cube
along with patterns arising from sucking a nipple. Upon
subsequent activation of the sucking scheme, that scheme
will be at the ready to assimilate aliment from a finger or a
cube as well as a nipple. So, through assimilation and accommodation of aliment a scheme conserves itself and also
modifies itself, i.e., it adapts. "All behavior is adaptation
and all adaptation is the establishment of equilibrium between the organism and its environment" (Piaget, 1981a,
p. 4).

Piaget's digestive model of the psyche, that is, his concept of assimilative and accommodative activity, provides
for active, holistic, equilibrated intrapsychic construction
as the basic developmental mode. This digestive model is
also an open system that allows for both maturational and
environmental influences. The scheme's assimilating and
accommodating as does a cell, organ, or organism provides for interaction of psychic structure with the external
environment. The digestive model provides a certain con-
servatism for the existing structure and yet allows for development. The model also allows for interaction between
biologic givens, such as reflexes, and the environment. It
suggests that the structure operates as a whole and when
possible takes in large patterned aliment. It is self-directed
in some measure, assimilating what it needs and allowing
the rest to pass it by.

We extrapolate Piaget's scheme to the clinical situation. Here a close parallel to Piaget's schemes would be the depth psychologist's use of complex; for example, Freud's Oedipus complex or Jung's animus, since one thinks of a complex as an abiding structured idiosyncratic approach to the world (Piaget, 1981a). In any particular person, schemes are the way that person is organized to interact with his world as he has constructed it.

The psyche as systems of schemes accounts for the syndromes we see in our daily practice, any abiding, i.e., repetitive configuration of conceptualization, percept or behavior, including symptoms or personalities. A clinical syndrome such as obsessive compulsive personality may be thought of as a scheme with its repetitive, hence abiding, activity. The obsessive traits of obstinacy, parsimony, and scrupulosity will be active in various settings much like a scheme. The syndrome not only repeats, but actively generalizes.

Even in the interpersonal and intrapsychic field the scheme as an abiding structure may be found. A young man urged his wife to see a psychiatrist, insisting that she needed help since she had had an affair with her boss. Accompanied by her husband, she came in very reluctantly. They agreed that initially she had not wished to work outside the home. He had insisted it would be good for them and for her if she worked. They could buy a home sooner, etc. At her first job she had an affair with her boss. Her husband had her leave that job and take another where she then had an affair with her new boss. She was interviewed only briefly alone. During that interview several points were clear. She resented being pushed by her husband to take a job. Now she felt competent in her work, had no particular interest in advancing in the job, but liked it, and planned to continue to work. She said her sex life with her husband was satisfactory—as was her sex life with her bosses. The husband telephoned later that night saying that they had had a pleasant early evening, but then subsequently they began to argue. She swallowed a number of pills. Unable to gain her cooperation in inducing vomiting, he stuck his finger down her throat, and she bit him. She refused to return for her next appointment. He, however, at the therapist's urging, did come in. During this appointment the therapist was able to point out that the wife was inclined to be passive, that the husband did things for her in order to help her or their relationship, and that she resented his pushing her around and would figuratively, or in this case literally, bite him. He seemed to understand this; but only when he reached the door and once again asked for the therapist's assistance in helping her to do a particular thing that would be good for her, did he seem to realize how automatic and repetitive his approach to her and her response to him was.

The scheme sustains itself and accommodates to new aliment. That is, the young man repeatedly coerces his wife to do what he thinks is best. His wife yields to pressure and then gets even when she has a chance. This broadened view of Piaget's schemes has treatment implications, especially where repetition compulsion and working through are concerned.

The tendency for certain symptoms or behaviors to persist or recur, Freud's transference phenomena or repetition compulsion, would seem to follow from viewing a syndrome as a scheme which is at the ready to assimilate familiar aliment and which accommodates to moderately different aliment whether that aliment is another lover or another authority figure. A clinical syndrome or the individual's own approach to different situations when viewed as a scheme readily fits the clinical finding that a single interpretation often is ineffective. The therapist (or patient) must often repeat an insight many times with minor variations on the theme before it takes effect. However, the tendency of the syndrome-as-scheme to assimilate and accommodate is consonant with the observation that therapists and patients alike may assimilate new and revolutionary insights, new aliment, again and again, make a slight twist of the aliment, accommodate, and not have their basic scheme change at all.

Consciousness and Unconsciousness

Returning to issues of the unconscious, we see that to the psychiatrically unsophisticated person unconscious processing is very mysterious, both in the style of data handling, for example, compressing two persons into one dream image (condensation), and in the fact that data are processed with little or no awareness. Consciousness or awareness surely is the greater mystery, however—not unconsciousness. Consciousness is the *something*; unconsciousness or unawareness is the absence of something. Something that is not there does not exist, and need not be explained. Consciousness, however, is as if it were a thing, a light that comes on, now shining here, now over there, sometimes brighter, sometimes dimmer. Piaget (1973) objected to this view of consciousness as a beacon that lit up dark corners. It is not the conceptualization that I will take, but such a concept does fit our everyday thinking of consciousness as a thing or an energy. In fact, by some, it is thought to transcend ourselves not only in three dimensions, but also in the fourth.

In its simplest terms we find ourselves taking the position that consciousness is an attribute of a set of schemes, much as red is an attribute of a particular scheme for a red ball. The understanding or construction of redness may be reduced to developing an understanding of activity occurring in a particular set of cones of the retina and their connections to the brain, and the patterns of activation (by the external world), as organized and reorganized over time as part of various schemes. Consciousness may be viewed as wakefulness. If redness at its most basic level is the activity in a certain set of retinal cones and their connections to the brain, then wakefulness is the relative state of activity in the system of neurons which connect the central nervous system with the peripheral motor and sensory nervous system (including the retinal cones). Thus, consciousness or wakefulness may be reduced to construction of an understanding of activity in the system of neurons of the sleep-wake centers and the patterns of activation as organized over time as part of various schemes, including schemes of the self and objects (i.e., as sense of alertness and of vividness).

Both Piaget and Freud agreed that most behavior is not controlled consciously, whether we are courting a mate, driving a car, or writing a word. The choice as to which systems monitor and lead to our next action or thought is not usually under conscious control. Imagine what a calamity it would be if we were constantly aware of our every sensation and our every move, plus the control systems involved. In fact, at times, some of our patients describe states in which they are overly aware of every nuance of meaning of the interactions they are engaged in, plus their entire surround. Such states are very disconcerting and disrupt ordinary function. Only as our function and its control are relegated to automaticity are we free to think about one of several things and free to try to deal with it. Yet, when we muster an argument and are functioning well, the smooth flow of expression testifies to a powerful and highly organized unconscious system directing what we become aware of as we give over to a system from somewhere inside us. Similarly, in psychotherapy, if the therapist does not interfere with the patient's free associations, then as the patient talks along, an underlying unconscious theme may be recognizable.

As noted, unconsciousness itself requires no explanation, any more than the unconsciousness of an automobile demands explanation except to children and primitives. Only the mechanics of unconscious process need be explained. Such mechanics were detailed by Freud. What generally goes unrecognized, however, is that Freud's description of these mechanics is meaningless without a backdrop of adult western logic. That is, when Freud pointed out that the unconscious uses condensation, displacement, and representation by opposites, these are significant deviations in thought process relative only to adult logical thought. Adult thought usually makes use of classification and seriation. Unconscious processes characterized by condensation, displacement, and representation by opposites use a kind of logic that Piaget calls preconceptual. This logic is typical of the two- to four-year-old, who not only fails to understand the relationship between class and subclass when dealing with attributes such as color or size, but also fails to understand gradedness of such attributes.

At two to four years of age, a preconceptual stage child fails to distinguish attributes from objects and thereby confounds one object with another. If he focuses on an attribute which two objects share, such as shape, he will assert that they are the same object. When Piaget's (1962a) daughter, Jacqueline, saw a slug on the path ten yards from a slug she had passed, she called it "the slug." Similarly, condensation betrayed in a slip will combine two individuals. For example, two colleagues, David Allen and Fred Alston, whom one thinks of as always having been very close to each other, may inadvertently be referred to as Dave Alston.

If a preconceptual-stage child focuses on an attribute of an object that is not usually coincident with that object, she may conclude that that same object is a different one. For example, Jacqueline declared that her sister Lucienne was not Lucienne when she was dressed in a new bathing suit and cap; then was Lucienne again when she was dressed in her usual clothes (Piaget, 1962a). This same type of failure in classification occurs in displacement (and condensation) in a symptom. For example, one patient's fear of crossing a bridge was a displacement of her fear of returning to a forbidden relationship with a man who lived on the other side of the bridge (plus return to her former life of prostitution).

Representation by opposites, that is, representation of an unconscious attitude by its opposite in consciousness, is illustrated by Freud's (1931) dream in which Goethe was criticized. The dream reversed Freud's resentment at Herr M.'s criticism of Freud's close friend. Such an example of reversal of configurations suggests that in the unconscious opposites are coded very closely together; as may be the case, for instance, with a black square and a white square, or with a patriot and a renegade. The thing or person and its activity are constituted by multidetermined schemes, made up of many attributes, some of which hold in a particular case while others do not. Prior to developing the ability to classify attributes, during the preoperational period two to seven years, black and white objects are not rigorously differentiated. It is not that a chld is unable to distinguish black from white, but when a two- to four-year-old is offered black and white squares and discs and asked to group the things that go together, he will likely make a figure, such as a train, out of a combination of the objects. A five- to seven-year-old has only an incipient notion of class and subclass which does not become rigorous until after he enters the concrete operational period (eight to twelve years).

The logic, the quality of classification of aliment by the child during the preconceptual stage (two to four years) and by unconscious mechanisms, is more of a "participation" (Piaget, 1962a, p. 226) of one thing with another than an embrace of class or subclass. It is rather assimilation of one similar scheme to another with very limited constraints. Likewise, wishes and words are as much a part of an event they refer to as the event itself. Jacqueline (Piaget, 1962a) was told it was too cold to go into a room where the garment she wanted was stored. After a short delay she announced that it was now warm and her garment could be gotten out. In a system such as the unconscious or in the preconceptual stage in which parts (attributes) and whole are not held separate, opposites are very close, separated by only a yes or no or a wish that it were not so.

In a system or a stage of development in which similarities and dissimilarities of attribute validate the presence or absence of an object, seriation of attributes cannot be rigorous. One cannot have a precise recognition of grades of color or grades of morality, for instance, badnesses and goodnesses. In Piaget's concrete operational period most children develop the ability to classify and seriate attributes, such as size, color, and moral good and bad. This ability to use rigorous classification and seriation, at least in the "thing" domain, is generally characteristic of their thought as adults.[4] It is only from this more mature system for viewing the world, a system which embraces class and subclass as well as gradedness, that unconscious data handling seems unusual or mysterious.

What we call deviations from the norm, then, the mechanisms and the characteristic logic of unconscious processing, are viewed as deviations only because of our western European adult frame of reference. When we appraise dreams, parapraxes, or symptoms, the windows through which we glimpse the unconscious cataloguing process, we remark how unusual that two things are put together that should be seen as distinct; or how unusual that one thing is represented by something else or by its opposite. We then postulate an unconscious system that arranges all these elements according to an "unusual" set of rules. The unusualness of the rules employed is of note only if we neglect our frame of reference, which employs the logic of concrete and/or formal operational cognition.

Since unconsciousness in itself is not a mystery which must be explained, the true mysteries, the true questions, are two: First, how does an organism starting out with such primitive and undifferentiated schemes as reflex schemes ever develop concrete and formal operational cognition? Second, what is consciousness?

In large measure, Piaget plotted the developmental sequence involved in a human being's truly remarkable construction of operational cognition. He also made certain suggestions regarding the mechanisms effecting the transformations of cognition from one stage to the next. My suggestions regarding the role of maturational factors in such transformations will be an important focus in this book.

As regards consciousness, Piaget's own explanation of formation of consciousness will not be accepted here, although his concepts regarding the dynamic control of awareness in a given situation will be adopted. With the aid of one of Freud's early hypotheses regarding the development of thought, I will draw heavily on Piaget's work to unravel the mystery of consciousness.

Notes

1. All ages are understood to be approximations.
2. Of course this parallel is not an absolute one. The delusions, misidentifications, and hallucinations of an adolescent who is schizophrenic necessarily will not manifest a thought disorder which is identical to the thought of a two- to four-year-old, since an adolescent's thought draws on quantitative and qualitative differences based on 10 additional years of maturation and experience. Also, the cognition typical of a two- to four-year-old

is manifest in both the physical and social domains while the cognition typical of a schizophrenic is essentially confined to the social domain.

3. I use "scheme" rather than "schema" for Piaget's "schème" as English translations did in his earlier texts. This is in keeping with Chilton's translation of Piaget and Inhelder's (1981) *Mental Imagery in the Child.* In that text Inhelder and Piaget used "schema" to designate only a "simplified model intended to facilitate presentation" (p. 367).

4. Some adults in certain areas of knowledge proceed to develop use of formal operations, classification of classification, or seriation of seriation. Most adults generally are at least able to use concrete operations, able to classify and seriate, although there remain some exceptions, at least in certain domains of knowledge (Bovet, 1976; Malerstein & Ahern, 1982).

Part I

A MODEL OF INTERPLAY BETWEEN MATURATION AND COGNITIVE DEVELOPMENT

Chapter 2

PIAGET'S STAGES OF COGNITIVE DEVELOPMENT

Before describing the interplay of brain development with cognitive development, this chapter will offer a sketch of Piaget's four periods of development to provide an orientation to theses that will follow. A major focus of this book is the sensorimotor period (0–2 years) to which we will return shortly.

The Four Periods

The second period of cognitive development, the preoperational period (two to seven years), has two stages: the preconceptual or symbolic stage (two to four years) and the intuitive stage (four to seven years).[1] As noted in Chapter 1, the preconceptual-stage child has a very limited understanding of separation of one object from another and virtually no understanding of separation of an object from its attributes. To Jacqueline her sister Lucienne in unusual clothes became another person. With a different attribute or part object (different clothes), sister was seen as a different object. Two objects with similar attributes, are thought to be one and the same object, as when Jacqueline became Clyde when she jumped as Clyde jumped (Piaget, 1962a).

In the next stage, the intuitive stage, the child understands that object and attribute are distinct from each other, but does not have a rigorous understanding of attributes. He may think the car that arrives first is the fastest car (Piaget,1954). He may think if you are punished you are bad (Piaget,1965) or if you are rewarded you are good (Kohlberg,1963). He has only an intuition of speed or morality. He is unable to classify or seriate objects in terms of their attributes. If he is collecting blue squares he may at some point include a blue disc in his collection. When arranging a series of different length sticks, he will violate the order at one point or another. He may place the sticks side by side, the tops of the sticks forming an ascending staircase, but disregard the bottom of the sticks, allowing them to form a ragged line rather than a straight horizontal one.

In the next period, the concrete operational period (seven to twelve years), a child is able to order a set of objects according to a plan, e.g., starting with the smallest stick, then the next larger, etc. He has a complete understanding of seriation involving both the relationships of neighbors in a series and a grasp of the idea of an entire series. Similarly, he can classify rigorously, making use of class and subclass, inclusion and exclusion. While by the end of this period he is able to classify and seriate objects in accordance with almost all attributes, certain attributes are understood first. He understands amount before weight, and color before length.

Finally, in the formal operational period (twelve years), which, as already mentioned, is not a universally attained cognitive level in all domains (e.g., morality or physics), the adolescent is able to classify classifications or seriate seriations. He can consider whether the greater moral good under particular circumstances may be to break a rule, e.g., to be dishonest. He may think about thinking, not just things. He may entertain the possible or hypothetical and reason from there. He may consider and test all the parameters that could influence the oscillation frequency of a pendulum.

Since the sensorimotor period is of special significance to the positions taken in this book, a brief description of each of its six stages will be offered. In stage 1 (0-1 month), the child practices his reflexes. He becomes better at sucking and grasping. His mouth adapts to the nipple or finger. Put another way, his sucking scheme accommodates to and assimilates sensorimotor aliment of the nipple and finger.

In understanding Piaget's constructivist system it is essential to understand that the scheme of an object is the object to the child. The sucking scheme, for example, to the neonate is the object he is sucking. It will be out of organizations and reorganizations of such scheme activity in interaction with his environment that the child constructs his world of space, time, and objects, including the self. If a stage-1 child is sucking on a wooden block, however organized by the sucking scheme including the sucking scheme's own particular history, the aliment consisting of the way the mouth is shaped, the failure of hunger satiation, the touch sensations from a hard angular object, all are the sucking scheme and all are the block to the child.

Such a primitive scheme of the block is hardly differentiated, hardly distinctive, at all. This sucking scheme activity is not separate from past sucking scheme activity made up of relatively different patterns, such as aliment derived from soft surfaces, rounded edges, warmth from an adjacent body, even sensations of satiation. It must also be realized that in these early stages the sucking scheme's parameters when sucking the block are the self as well as the block. So, to begin with, the child has present-past self-objects.

Circular Reactions

Both stages 2 (two to four months) and 3 (five to eight months) are characterized by circular reactions, that is, the repetition of adventitious actions. Stage 2 is characterized by primary circular reactions. For example, when making a striking movement, if a child encounters a blanket edge with his palm, he may repeat his movements, grasping and letting go, grasping and letting go, for 15 minutes at a time (Piaget, 1963). Based on observation of such behavior Piaget inferred that the child's striking scheme was being assimilated to his grasping scheme and vice versa. Similarly, a child may be observed to extrude and suck on his tongue over and over. In this example, protrusion-of-the-tongue scheme and sucking scheme mutually assimilate each other. In contrast to stage 2, in which the child's sensory focus is primarily proximal, for instance touch, in stage 3 the child's sensory focus becomes distal, for instance visual. He repeats adventitious actions that give rise to watching or listening. This is called a secondary circular reaction. For example, when Lucienne in stage 3 struck a suspended doll with her foot and caused it to bounce, she watched the movement of the doll as she repeatedly struck it with her foot (controlling it tactually without looking at her foot) (Piaget, 1963, p. 159). One may not infer that she understands the causal relationship between her foot striking and the doll's bouncing, but merely that her striking scheme is assimilated to her watching scheme and her watching scheme is assimilated to her striking scheme. Similarly, Laurent listened to the sound he made as he repeatedly rubbed a piece of paper against a wicker surface

(Piaget, 1963, p. 169). His hand-movement scheme is assimilated to his listening scheme and vice versa.

Also, having rolled his head or struck with his foot and caused the movement of a mobile attached to his crib, a child varies his own particular repertoire of movements, such as shaking his legs, striking with his arm, arching his back, rolling his head, besides varying the vigor of his movements as he watches the mobile move more, less, or not at all. These scheme variations are assimilated to each other, to a greater or lesser extent, the extent being a function of his present and past experience and any prewired organic constraints according to whether his foot or his head-rolling motion is used.

In the first three sensorimotor stages with one exception there is no clear evidence that one scheme is distinguished from another while both schemes are simultaneously active. The schemes and their variations are mutually assimilated. Though they differ in significance and frequency, all of the parameters and their variations are part of the same scheme as the child strikes while watching and watches while striking.

When a child strikes the doll with his foot while watching, he does not understand the necessity of contact between his foot and the doll (Piaget, 1963, p. 160). When the doll was held up above Jacqueline's face, outside range of contact with her foot, she went through her repertoire of movements. To the extent that a child does not understand a causal connection between one object and another or one activity and another, he also does not make a separation between objects. There is no reason to assume that he distinguishes the self-striking from the doll-bouncing. In stage 3, object schemes are merged. When a stage-3 child encounters a novel object, after showing momentary surprise, he incorporates that object into his usual activity schemes, striking with his foot, shaking his head, making a

rubbing movement; "the younger the child, the less novel-
ties seem new to him" (Piaget, 1963, p. 196). So, self, object, and other objects are not differentiated from one another in stage 3.

It is of special interest that stage 4 (eight to twelve
months), in contrast to earlier stages, manifests beginning
separation of one simultaneously active scheme from another. In stage 4, in order to grasp a watch, a child may be
observed to knock aside and later to set aside an intervening pillow (Piaget, 1963). To some extent, his pillow
scheme is differentiated from his watch scheme, and his
striking scheme or picking-up scheme from his grasping
scheme. One object is beginning to be separate from another and one activity of the self from another.

The only evidence we have for early differentiation of
one subscheme from another is of hunger-gratification
sucking schemes and hunger-non-gratification sucking
schemes. A month-old, hungry child, if offered a finger to
suck, quickly rejects it. If he is not hungry he will suck either a finger or nipple. With this exception,[1] until stage 4
(eight to twelve months) there is no evidence of differentiated articulations between simultaneously active schemes.
Prior to stage 4, two simultaneously active schemes are either a finger or nipple. With this exception,[2] until stage 4
scheme. In stage 4, when a child strikes a pillow to get it
out of the way in order that he may grasp a watch, there is
evidence of a temporal ordering of schemes, a differentiation of past and present schemes, that is, striking before
grasping. The pillow scheme is somewhat separate from
the watch scheme. The striking-pillow scheme of the self is
somewhat distinct from the grasping-watch scheme of the
watch. Yet, as will be seen, the self and object of stage 4 are
clearly still self-object; objects, including the self, are not
separate from each other except in limited ways.

Nevertheless, the important point is that such distinctions have begun. Also, Piaget showed that in steps such

separations become better defined until stage 6 (about eighteen months of age) of the sensorimotor period when object schemes, including the schemes of the self, are at times fully separate from one another. In stage 6 a child successfully searches behind any number of screens for an object. If it is hidden behind a pillow and, unseen by the child, placed under a beret which was already hidden under the pillow, he will generally search under the beret. Behavior such as this allowed Piaget to infer that the pillow scheme, the beret scheme, and the watch scheme are separate from each other and from the self scheme; that in stage 6 a child has object schemes that are separate from other object schemes.

Changing Relationships Between Schemes

Differentiation of one object from another, while begun in stage 4, is far from complete. If one places a matchbox on a book, although the child is initially interested in the matchbox, he will not reach for it (Piaget, 1954, p. 177). He may reach for the book instead. The object and the platform schemes merge. Yet, under certain circumstances the object schemes are distinct from one another. If the platform is much larger, if it constitutes a "neutral base" (Piaget, 1954, p. 182), the child will reach for the matchbox. If the matchbox slides on the book, he will reach for the matchbox. If the object is on a pedestal, e.g., a goblet (p. 177), the child will reach for it. Although separations of one object scheme from another remain restricted to certain configurations, stage 4 marks the inception of a new kind of relationship between schemes which continues at least through stage 6 (when object schemes are at times fully separate from one another). In stage 4, no longer is one scheme merely assimilated to another. Rather, a coordination of one scheme with another takes place (Piaget, 1963). Each coordination helps differentiate one object scheme from another. In striking a pillow in order to grasp a watch, one scheme is active first, the other second. One is more distant, farther to reach, than the other. All these constitute distinctions between schemes and yet each coordination unites these same schemes in a particular relationship.

In stage 5 (twelve to sixteen months) the child will reach for an object as it rests motionless on a platform. In fact, he will use the platform, such as a cushion, to pull the watch to him, if the watch is out of reach and the platform is not. While stage 5 is marked by extention of differentiations of schemes for different objects, there is still reason to believe that to the stage-5 child the watch and cushion schemes are not entirely separate from each other.

To understand the child's level of recognition of separateness of objects, examination of her searching for a hidden object at each stage is instructive. In stage 3 if, before the child's eyes, an experimenter places an object under a screen, for instance, hides her bottle under a pillow, in order for her to search for the hidden object part of the object must show. If her bottle is fully hidden under a pillow, she will cease reaching for the bottle unless she was already making a grasping movement with her hand, or unless her hand had already grazed the bottle. In stage 4, she will search under the pillow for the hidden bottle. But if she successfully recovers her bottle under a pillow on her right and if, while she watches, her bottle is hidden under a pillow on her left, she will tend to search under the pillow on her right. In stage 5 she will search under the screen where she last saw the object disappear, rather than where she had successfully retrieved the object in the past. Still, we may not conclude that for her the object is separate from the screen behind which she sees the object disappear. For if a beret is hidden under the pillow without her knowing it and if, unseen by her, the object once passed under the pillow is hidden under the beret, her search will usually stop short of looking under the beret. The object is, in effect, part of the first screen behind which it passes. In stage 6, however, the child will search under any number of hidden screens. In order to search behind a second screen, such as the beret, she must have a scheme of the object which is distinct from any of the screens.

Indexing

Use of indices, an achievement of stage 4, illustrates the lack of differentiation of schemes and the use to which this undifferentiation is put. For example, when mother put on her hat, indicating her imminent departure, Jacqueline (eleven months) cried (Piaget, 1962a, p. 250). Mother's hat was used by Jacqueline as an index. She has somewhat separate schemes for mother-with-hat and mother-without-hat. Mother-with-hat-leaves; mother-without-hat-stays. There is no reason to assume, however, that the mother scheme and the hat scheme are separate from each other. It is probable that it is this attachment of the two objects to the whole situation of departure, including the affect involved, which permits the observer to think of the child as using an index.[3]

The type of indexing found in stage 4 is a failure in differentiation, a sort of leftover from stage 3. It is consonant with the tendency for schemes to assimilate any aliment that is coincident in time with the activity of the scheme. The hat is not differentiated from mother any more than the matchbox is differentiated from the book. This position is also consistent with evidence that until four years of age, objects may be merged or multiple-based upon a change in a part of the object (See the first page of this chapter), and that object and symbol (e.g., word) have very fuzzy boundaries (Piaget, 1962a).

The progress of imitation in the sensorimotor period as observed by Piaget (1962a) helps to illustrate further the use of indices, another aspect of the lack of differentiation between object schemes and the use to which the child puts this undifferentiation. In stage 3, a child, having become adept at striking a hanging object, such as a doll, and causing it to swing, may not bother to strike the object, but merely imitate its swinging movement (or merely make an aborted striking motion, an imitation of the self). If the experimenter blinks his eye, the child may open and close his fist, imitating the blinking configuration. Such stage-3 imitation is almost a contagion, with one previously related subscheme activated by the present one or with a present one being assimilated to a similar configuration. In stage 3 a child is unable to imitate using a part of himself which he cannot see.[4] For example, if the experimenter sticks out his tongue, unless the child has just stuck out his tongue, he does not imitate the experimenter. If the child sticks out his tongue and the experimenter imitates the child, the child will stick out his tongue and a dialogue may be set up, each imitating the other. A day later, if the experimenter sticks out his tongue, the child will not.

In stage 4, however, if, as the child is sticking out his tongue, he also makes a bubbling sound and if the experimenter imitates both the tongue movement and the sound, not only is a dialogue set up; but also, later, without use of the bubbling sound as an index, the child will imitate the experimenter whenever he sticks out his tongue (Piaget, 1962a). (The imitation may not be precise, it may be a pressing of his lips together, but imitation is clearly intended.) This imitation without use of the bubbling sound may be elicited days later. Initially the sound is used as an index, as noted above, and is a part of a scheme which also contains subschemes of movement of the tongue and watching (acting on with the eyes) the experimenter's tongue movement. Later, the index is abandoned.

In stage 5, an index is no longer necessary in order for

a child to find a part of his face he cannot see (Piaget, 1962a). The child will directly imitate a movement he cannot see and has not performed before, but with some initial groping. That is, he may approximate sticking out his tongue and then correct himself till he does the task. It is much like other behavior in stage 5. If inadvertently he causes a matchbox to flip by pressing on its edge, he will press on the box here and there, experimenting until he learns what he must do to master flipping the box. All the groping subactivities are part of the primary activity, imitation of a hidden mouth movement or of causing the box to flip.

Finally, in stage 6, he will imitate an activity he has never seen or done before, even after a day's delay (Piaget, 1962a). Having never seen the warming motion of striking the body with the arms, Jacqueline (sixteen months) imitated Piaget immediately without any groping. Having never had a temper tantrum herself, Jacqueline (sixteen months) with some laughter imitated one that she had observed the day before. So, in stage 6 there is not necessarily any groping, no behaviorally evident index connected to imitating new activities. The earlier stage-4 and 5- "failures" in separation of one object scheme from another are instrumental in advancing imitation and experimentation to stage 6 where such undifferentiations are, at times, dispensed with. The failures of separation are at once instruments of progress and leftovers of undifferentiation. (Are such failure-instruments anlage of language?)

Source of the Scheme

We have just emphasized certain aspects of Piaget's conceptualization of the schemes of the sensorimotor period which are critical for the positions to be taken in this book. That, as undifferentiated as a scheme is to begin with, to the child such a scheme is the object (and the self) and that out of this scheme, given certain maturational factors and interactions with the environment, the child is able to construct a differentiated world of objects including his self as an object.

What is a scheme? Is it just a hypothetical construct, some theoretical structure that has an embryologic-like history and a digestive system-like means of sustaining and adapting itself? Or may a scheme be reduced to an organic, material substrate, either neurophysiologic or biochemical activity or some combination of the two? Does the scheme have any identifiable substrate in the brain?

Piaget approached these questions very cautiously. It is clear that he thought there was a relationship between his schemes and the brain, although he did not settle on whether the scheme resides in a neuronal configuration (Piaget, 1971) or whether it is located somewhere at the chromosomal level (Piaget & Inhelder 1973).

Taking a less cautious approach, I suggest that the scheme is a particular pattern of activity of neuronal circuits. There obviously is some relationship between the schemes and biochemicals, such as neurotransmitters and neurotransmitter production, and perhaps RNA and other cellular chemicals. But the scheme and scheme interrelationships can be seen to be isomorphic to neuronal circuitry.

A general position of Piaget's was that schemes are not passive, but are active and interactive in constructing better equilibrated understandings of the world and the self. The implication is that, while requiring nutrient, once a scheme is established, it is stimulus-seeking, has its own tendency to sustain itself, and is also actively selective, assimilating only kinds of aliment that approximate previous aliment. We may translate these qualities into neurophysiological terms.

A Neurophysiological Concept of Schemes

For many years it has been assumed that neuronal circuits, once activated, are more readily reactivated and further that this increased tendency to be reactivated is a function of changes in synaptic junctions. Recently some of the mechanisms of this "memory" of a neuronal circuit have been elucidated. Altered calcium metabolism (Kandel, 1979) and production of peptide cotransmitters (Coyle, 1985) in the presynaptic neuron as well as up or down regulation of the receptors of the post-synaptic neuron (Sulzer et al, 1984 and Louie, 1985) are all mechanisms in which activation results in modulating the synapse's, hence its circuit's, tendency to be reactivated. These biochemical changes involved in such "learning" at the synapse may, however, vary from one species to another and from one brain region to another. Nevertheless, "change in the strength of connections between neurons" being involved in learning as proposed by Ramon y Cajal (and Freud) in 1894, appears likely (Klein, Shapiro and Kandel, 1980). Another finding that is consonant with this position is that the presynaptic knobs, which store and release neurotransmitter substances into the synaptic cleft, are in great abundance to begin with, but diminish with maturity (Jacobsen, 1975). It is thought that the plethora of knobs provides a great redundancy in the less mature organism and that the knobs which survive to maturity are those which are repeatedly used. Hence, there is a fixity of certain circuits, based upon their use.

We think of the sucking reflex as a prewired neuronal circuit, built-in prior to birth, so that stimulation in the area of the mouth activates it, and once activated, it will tend to be more easily reactivated. If, to begin with, the sucking scheme coincides with activity in the neural circuitry of the sucking reflex, then when the reflex is repetitively active, since much of the central nervous system is interconnected, many other neuron sets corresponding to other systems active at the same time (e.g., sensations of warmth from the mother's body, tactile sensations generated by the hardness of the object sucked, etc.) will very quickly feed into the sucking scheme. This would amount to the scheme's assimilation of aliment. If the warmth of the mother's body or the hardness of the block is coincident with the sucking reflex activity frequently enough, then these neuronal activities will be enough of a part of the sucking circuitry that the circuitry will be modified to readily respond to, that is, accommodate, this type of aliment.

Once this sucking neuronal circuit scheme is entrenched and has its particular established components because of its particular history, then this circuit stands at the ready whenever there is diffuse activity of the central nervous system—more than some less entrenched scheme or than some random configuration of activity. Thus the sucking circuit scheme will connect to, take in, new activity. It will appear to be an active assimilator, running its own show, stimulus seeking. It is of course also active in the sense of selective, responding more to some types of aliment, some types of circuit activity, than it does to others. The circuit-scheme is also holistic. The holism of the initial circuit schemes reflects the basic initial undifferentiation of the circuitry of the central nervous system. This globality is not total even in the beginning, since one does not elicit a grasping reflex by touching the mouth or a sucking reflex by touching the palm of the hand. Nevertheless, the diffuse connectedness of different networks of neurons is considerable and only with learning and maturation are increasing restraints applied as to what scheme will assimilate what aliment, what circuit will connect to another, under what circumstances and in what order.

Let us now consider how such a neuron circuit view of

schemes relates to Piaget's notion that the child actively constructs his own world. How is he building it? The mature organism understands the color red as a range of redness, and as distinct from blue. Without retinal cones that respond to electromagnetic waves of a particular frequency the child could not see red. Likewise, if he lived in a blue world, if our atmosphere acted like a filter which would not allow red light to pass through it, he could not see red. So to construct redness he must have both red light and retinal cones that respond to red light.

But what does a young child know about red light? He merely has retinal cones that respond to a certain frequency range of light and other cones that respond to different frequencies. Due to prewiring, these different sets of cones connect to different sets of neurons in the central nervous system. The activity of these sets of neurons, the pre-red scheme, are redness to the child, though he does not know what to call it; though it is not yet red balls, cars, or skies; though it is certainly not redness differentiated from the balls, cars, and skies; though it will be built by experience with such objects; and though the pre-red scheme set of neurons is not separate from many other connections to these neurons which are unrelated to redness. At some point this activity in the brain coming from this specific set of cones will be redness, redness distinct from objects and redness distinct from other attributes including other colors.

Essentially, when one constructs an understanding of redness, one is merely constructing an understanding of one's own retinal cones (as over time their activity interacts with other nervous system activity, especially eye and neck muscle proprioception). In a strange way, that is all we really study and know, parts of our own nervous system and how these parts respond to the activities of other parts of our nervous system. From these we imagine, construct, an external world and self.

Notes

1. The intuitive and preconceptual stages were regarded by Piaget as phases, not clearly ordered or demarcated stages (Inhelder, personal communication).

2. It might be argued that these schemes are not simultaneously active.

3. The position taken here is consistent with Piaget's findings, but is not one that was proposed by him. Piaget merely emphasized that the index scheme of stage 4 was separate from some ongoing activity. I am detailing how it is separate and how it is not.

4. Although the child imitates activities such as tongue protrusion shortly after birth, these responses fade (Maratos, 1973).

Chapter 3

THE ROLE OF THE VISUAL CORTEX IN CONSTRUCTION OF OBJECTNESS

Piaget proposed that the fundamental factors in cognitive development are social experience, maturation, physical experience, and equilibration (Gallagher & Reid, 1981). Equilibration he defines as a "search for better and better equilibrium" (Piaget, 1981b p. 219). He addressed social experience and maturation in more limited fashion than he did the other two. Earlier we addressed a basic aspect of social experience in our clinical study of character syndromes and their relationship to cognitive development (Malerstein & Ahern, 1982). In this chapter I shall present a model of how a maturational factor induces cognitive development.

Equilibration

Piaget, in his efforts to understand development, took what Gallagher and Reid (1981) refer to as the middle ground, taking neither the position of the empiricist, emphasizing learning, nor that of the innatist, emphasizing maturation. Piaget's position was that the child is a self-regulating, i.e., equilibrating, organism which interacts with the external world and actively constructs its schemes of the self and the world. Piaget carefully distinguished equilibrium or equilibration in cognitive structures from equilibrium in chemistry or physics. In the case of a chemical reaction or of a balance scale, equilibrium reaches a static end point. In cognition, equilibrium is a dynamic balance which moves toward higher levels of organization. Piaget (1981b) described three types of cognitive equilibrium, one between assimilation and accommodation, another between subsystems of the subject's schemes, and a third equilibrium between the parts of the subject's knowledge and the totality of his knowledge. Piaget (p. 219) hypothesized that this third type of equilibrium is "probably the secret of development and of the transition from one stage to the next."

Piaget (1981b) acknowledged that in the very early stages of the sensorimotor period, as for example when the child coordinates grasping with vision, the prime factor in development is the maturational one, that is myelination of neural tracts. However, he draws on equilibration as the prime stimulus to higher organizations. Representative and operational cognitive structures "are not innate" (p. 214). He proposed that the maturational factor operates in cognitive development as an inductor influences restructuring in a developing embryonic tissue. If the inductor is present too early or too late it has little or no effect. The tissue must do the responding and must be at a particular state of competence.

The concepts I will present are completely in keeping with a notion of the organic factor operating as an inductor, which, when the cognitive organization is ready, induces cognition to reorganize itself. Oddly enough, our earlier work is consonant with an inductor-like maturational factor providing the opportunity to form stable character structures, but not dictating type, the type being a function of the child's reaching an equilibrium between his constructs of the self and of his social world (Malerstein & Ahern, 1982).

The model I propose is neither empiricist nor innatist, but one which conserves Piaget's interactionist, constructivist position.

Myelination

Committed as Piaget was to biology, he nevertheless left a large unbridged gap between psychological development, namely, his cognitive stages, and the organic substrate. In chapters 5 and 6 I will show how consciousness may be understood in terms of the mechanics of the developing nervous system parcelled out by cognitive development. In this chapter I present an explicit theory of the relationship between brain development and Piaget's stages of cognitive development, particularly stage 4 of the sensorimotor period. I show how bringing on-line the function of a particular brain structure through myelination can induce the type of cognitive processing that begins in Piaget's stage 4.

The focus of this chapter is the visual system, because we now have improved understanding of the neurophysiology of the subsystems of the visual system. The model proposed embodies a type of interplay between the physiology and psychology of the organism which in its general format may apply to neural organizations other than the visual system. The proposal links three areas of investigation, neurophysiology, developmental anatomy, and cognitive development. The focus will be visual data processing by the primary visual area of the cortex, area 17, as explained by Hubel and Weisel (1979). Their work suggests that the cells of the visual cortex have a filtering or gating function. As a function of the patterns of visual stimulation to the eye, visual sensory data coming to area 17 are transmitted differentially to cells beyond area 17. I propose that myelination of the geniculocalcarine tract (the last segment to be myelinated of the major tract connecting the retina to area 17) brings on-line area 17. Further, I propose that the particular criteria which area 17 employs for information-gating play a major role in the sighted child's ability to differentiate one object from another. Such differentiation of one object from another begins in Piaget's stage 4.

Confirmation of this proposal, that myelination of the geniculocalcarine tract plays a basic role in stage-4 function, depends on the timing of myelination of the tract relative to onset of stage-4 cognition. Unfortunately, we have as yet no direct measures of stage-4 behavior correlating either with myelination to area 17 or with area 17 activity (though such measures are now possible, with the advent of the PET or MR scan). Nonetheless, the work of Lecours (1975) and Yakovlev, who charted the myelination of a number of pathways of the developing nervous system, makes it appear likely that complete myelination of fibers from the eye to area 17 takes place just before stage 4 begins. Lecours and Yakovlev found that the fibers that connect the retina to the lateral geniculate ganglion, the ganglion cell fibers, begin myelination in the ninth fetal month and are completely myelinated during the third or fourth postnatal month. The fibers of the geniculocalcarine tract, which connect the lateral geniculate ganglion to the visual cortex, begin myelination two weeks before birth and are completely myelinated at the end of the fourth or fifth month.

A child is concluding stage 3 and ready to enter stage 4 when myelination of the tract to area 17 is complete, at about six months of age. According to Piaget (1973) stage 4 begins at about eight months of age, but according to more recent studies (Spelke, in Press) (and in Piaget's (1963) son, who exhibited stage 4 behavior at six months) it begins somewhat earlier. Of course, the proposed onset of a sensorimotor stage is approximate, just as is a date for completion of myelination of fibers of the geniculocalcarine tract. Nonetheless, it is almost certain that myelination of the geniculocalcarine tract is not complete prior to stage 3 (four to eight months) and yet must be complete before stage 5 (twelve to eighteen months). So it is reasonable to view myelination of the optic tract from the eye to area 17 as a usual antecedent to stage-4 function.

If area 17 is brought on-line just before stage 4 begins, area 17's becoming operative may prepare for stage 4 function. Then we must ask, how would the operation of area 17 feed into stage 4? Hubel and Weisel's (1979) work provides an answer. Using microelectrodes and recording from single cells, Hubel and Weisel found that cells of area 17 (except for the cells of layer IV, which appear to be the final stop for the geniculocalcarine tract) of the monkey responded maximally when the monkey's eye was stimulated by a line of light at a particular angle. One such cell responded maximally to a bright line with a dark surround cast on the retina, another to a dark line with a bright surround, another to a boundary between darkness and light, and another to lines of light when they moved across the retina. Other cells respond maximally to binocular light stimulation. Also of importance is the distribution of cells' differential responsiveness, which is orderly within blocks of the visual cortex, such blocks corresponding to areas of the retina. This correspondence suggests that the relationship between configurations of line stimulation is conserved as the stimulation passes from the eye to the occipital cortex.

In contrast, the cells anterior to area 17, the ganglion cells of the retina and the cells that make up the geniculocalcarine tract, plus the cells of layer IV of area 17, do not respond differentially to lines of light or to binocular stimulation. Rather, these cells, which are the conduit for visual data transmission from the eye to area 17, are maximally active when the retina is stimulated by spots of light with a dark surround or spots of darkness with a light surround.

Gating

Given the differential responsiveness of the cells of area 17, area 17 could be expected to function like a filter, like a set of highly selective gates. A particular area-17 cell is more likely to fire, that is, to pass information through it to cells further downstream in the visual system, depending upon the pattern of light stimulating the retina. The particular angle of a line of light cast on the retina and whether the line is moving or not will select which area-17 cell will fire. Each cell of area 17 probably has specific axonal connections downstream deeper into the brain. Hence, depending on which cells of area 17 are active, only certain downstream cells will be activated. Thus as a function of the orientation of the lines and edges of light cast upon the retina, and of whether these lines of light move or not, only certain cells beyond area 17 will be activated.

Such distinctions of lines of light or boundaries between a light and dark region which I will call an edge of light would assist differentiation of one object from another, based on the different orientations of each object's boundaries or edges and on whether these lines and edges move as a set. For example, the sets of cells that are maximally active beyond area 17 could be expected to be quite different for a compound line such as ⎯⎯/ compared to one shaped like ⎯⎯\ . Irrespective of modest differences in size identically shaped closed figures, including objects, in the same orientation and with the correspond-

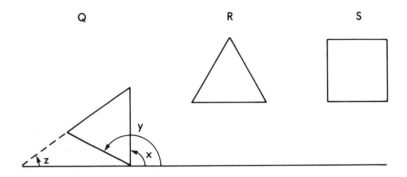

Figure 1

ing edge of each figure having the same quality (light line, dark line, or edge, movement or not) could be expected to yield a pattern of activity beyond area 17 that is basically the same. Whether the image of an object cast upon the retina is somewhat larger or smaller, provided the image is the same configuration of lines and edges, the same basic set of area-17 cells would probably fire, giving rise to the same patterns of activity beyond area 17. Those patterns of stimulation coming from the same object would be filtered as the same, that is, would be passed on together as a set, as the object moves closer to or further from the eye, even though a larger or smaller image might be cast on the retina. Not differentiating an object's image on the retina when distance from the eye to the object changes, supports coding such variations in image size as belonging to the same object (scheme). Even a foreshortening of the figure on one axis (looking at an object from an angle) would be passed through, gated, as similar to the nonforeshortened figure. Most of the same cells of area 17 would be maximally stimulated. Hence, the same patterns of activity of nerve cells central to area 17 may also be expected to be the same. See Figure 1.

If the lines of light cast upon the retina by the edges of an object Q are at angles x, y, and z, then object Q is probably present when the corresponding cells, X, Y, and Z of area 17, are simultaneously active. At least Q is more likely present than when a different set of cells is active, for instance, cells corresponding to lines or edges of light reflected off object R or object S. It is interesting that if the set of lines or edges is rotated, then the cells of area 17 that are activated would be quite different; hence the stimulation patterns beyond area 17 would be different. If Q is rotated (so that it appears like R) very different cells in area 17 and beyond would be activated. Hence, initially, in stage 4, Q is coded as quite a different pattern when it is rotated. However, in late stage 4 (page 61) and in stage 5 (page 103), one focus of the child's study is rotation of edges. A stage-5 child learns by assimilation and accommodation, not by conditioning, that is, he discovers that he is successful with a rotated as well as a nonrotated set of edges. He can do with a rotated set of edges, R, whatever he likes to do with a nonrotated set, Q. He learns their difference from object S, whose shape is basically different, whose edges have a different set of angles. While a stage-5 child learns that sets of lines and edges which rotate are still the same object, to the stage-4 child, rotation of an object, rotation of a set of lines and edges, would still blur the distinction of that object from another object, and from any other set of lines and edges. (It will be evident later that we may infer that, while the transition from stage 3 to 4 appears to be induced by a maturational factor, transition from stage 4 to stage 5 may rest primarily on reequilibration, that is on learning or discovery.)

When the eye is subject to lines of light at various angles, the differential response of area 17 cells is not due to an inherent tendency of these cells to recognize such stim-

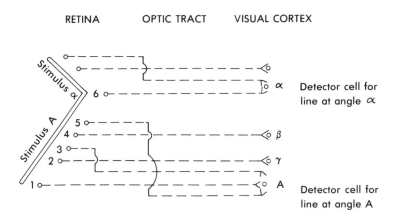

Figure 2

Schematic of a line of retinal cells to their circuit's convergence on a visual cortex cell.

ulation patterns, since area 17 cells are much like any other neurons. Rather, these cells' differential responsiveness to patterns of stimulation is due to the wiring that is (embryologically) built into the visual nervous system. See Figure 2 for a possible schematic of such wiring. If retinal cells, which are positioned in a straight line, connect (through several relay stations) to other cells whose fibers converge upon cell A in the visual cortex, then, when the retinal cells which are in that line fire, a number of stimuli will simultaneously impinge on cell A. Cell A then will tend to fire more readily than its neighbors. It is in this manner that an area 17 cell could act as a gate.

Suppose that a line of light is cast upon retinal cells 1, 3, and 5 in Figure 2, whose fibers converge on the area 17 cell, cell A, before the fibers connecting the retina to area 17 are myelinated. Then the stimuli transduced by the light could be expected merely to drift in to area 17. The corresponding line stimulus, stimulus A, will not be much more effective in triggering its gate cell, A, than it would other cells, such as alpha, beta, and gamma. While the same line stimulus stimulates A, it activates cells 2, 4, and 6, but the fibers of cells 2, 4, and 6 do not converge on one area-17 cell.

The gating action of area 17 is not functional before the nerve fibers coming to it are myelinated. Although the primary function of myelin is merely to speed transmission of impulses, information is less useful if it is transmitted in an untimely fashion. In a system which is dependent upon summation of nearly simultaneous impulses, as is the case with the nervous system, information may fail to be effective at all if it is delayed. Also, without myelination, stimuli may be diffused or lost due to the absence of the insulating quality of myelin. We may assume that without sufficient myelination of afferent fibers to a unit in the nervous system (and perhaps beyond that unit), the unit is not truly functional. We may assume, then, that area 17 is not on-line, does not carry out its basic role, before the tracts to it are myelinated. Of course, this does not mean that once afferent fibers are myelinated that the unit which these fibers serve is now in full operation. It merely means that the usual function of this unit may begin to be part of the system.

Prior to myelination of the geniculocalcarine tract, transmission of data to area 17 and beyond could be expected to take place, but in the absence of gate cell function the data would not be as differentially located; hence, the information would not be as differentially patterned beyond area 17. Prior to myelination of the tract to area 17, only visual data differentiated in terms of bright center and dark surround and vice versa (based on the gating action of the cells which are anterior to the cortex) could be expected to reach the brain in a timely fashion. Such differential responsiveness or gating might conceivably be used to help differentiate one object from another, but only minimally, on the basis of overall difference in the brightness of different objects. Such differentiation would be no more precise than that offered by differential response to color. Certain objects under certain lighting conditions may be differentiated on the basis of color or light and dark, but many may not. Boundaries read from lines or edges of light that move as a set provide much better parameters for constructing objectness.

Our points thus far are twofold: (1) that cells of area 17 allow passage of visual data based upon whether those data are in the form of a line or edge at a particular angle and/or whether the line or edge is moving across the retina or not; (2) that a requirement for bringing the cells of area 17 on-line, hence for their line/edge-movement gating function, is myelination of the visual tract to area 17.

Stage-4 Cognition

Let us consider the organization of cognition in stage 4, and how a line/edge-movement gating mechanism might serve this level of cognition. Recall that, in contrast to earlier stages, stage 4 evidences a beginning separation of one object scheme from another simultaneously active object scheme. Nonetheless, if one places an object, such as a matchbox, on a platform, the stage-4 child will not reach for it. He may reach for the platform instead. The object and platform schemes merge. If the platform is much larger, the child will reach for the object. If the object slides on the platform, he will reach for the object.[1] If the object is on a pedestal, he will reach for it. So in stage 4, while there is clear evidence for the first time that the child distinguishes one object scheme from another, such distinctions remain limited.

How does having a line-edge/movement gating system, area 17, operating serve this new ability to separate one object scheme from another? Clearly, movement of the matchbox relative to its platform displays the matchbox's lines or edges, its boundaries. Movement (of the set of edges or lines of the matchbox), in itself, is a critical factor in the child's being able to separate one object from another, for movement of a set of lines is a more telltale indicator of an edge of an object than are stationary lines. A cell that responds maximally to movement of sets of lines selects the most significant visual aliment for construction of separate schemes for objects which are themselves distinct from each other. In the case of an object on a pedestal, most of the set of edges of the object is separate from the platform's set of edges. In the case of the larger platform, we do not know if the platform must be so large that its boundaries are not in the same field of vision as the object. In these examples, and in cases where the edges of objects are fully separate, as when the child strikes the pillow to gain access to the watch, construction of separation between object schemes would be aided by a system which responds differentially to the orientation of a set of edges or lines and their movement as a set.

In stage 4, while, as pointed out, differentiation of one object from another is limited to certain conditions, the important points are that the child for the first time demonstrates that he distinguishes between one object and another, and that such object differentiation is consistent with the processing of sets of lines and edges and their movement. It is probably not happenstance that the fibers to area 17 are myelinated, that the line/edge-movement gating system is put into service, just before the system begins to be exploited in construction of objects.

Differentiation in Stage 5

In stage 5 the child's exploitation of edges in constructing his object world becomes more refined. In stage

4, for example, the child does not see that the closed outline of the matchbox is a separate object unless it starts to
slide as it rests on its platform. If the object is on a pedestal, only if most of its edges are separate from the platform's does the child treat a stationary object as separate.
In stage 5 a child reaches for an object, even though it is
not moving relative to the platform. He no longer needs
the edges of the matchbox to move relative to the platform's edges. Additionally, he exploits the connection represented by the small failure of separate edges between
two objects, for he pulls on a string in order to retrieve an
object. Now he should be able to reach for the stem of the
goblet.

In stage 5 a child studies an object's behavior as he
drops it and watches it fall or as he lets swing a suspended
object, such as a tie. In stage 4 such study of object behavior was confined to relationships to the self, such as bringing the object closer to the self, watching himself let go of
an object. As stage 4 continues, a child studies an object
from all views. He slowly rotates an object and moves it in
all three planes as he carefully watches it. He appears to be
capitalizing on his new edge-movement detector. Late in
stage 4, and subsequently, he knows how to find the reverse side of an object. If offered the non-nipple end of his
bottle, he will rotate the bottle. In stage 3 or early stage 4,
he must first have gotten a glimpse of the nipple before he
would rotate the bottle. In stage 5 he studies the changes
of objects relative to other objects as he stacks them or
causes them to topple, and he is able to place a thimble on
a table so it will not roll. Not until stage 6 does he understand nonpenetrability of object edges. In stage 5 he will
touch a ring to the side of a stick expecting it to surround
the stick or, having passed a hoop over his head, he will try
to pass a solid disk over his head. All of these extensions
of the know-how of objects could be seen as exploiting
object boundaries, as pushing to its limits the line/edge-
movement set detector monitored by success and failure,

whether the measure of success is assimilation to a scheme or whether it is alleviation of hunger.

Returning to the stage-4 example of removing a pillow in order to get a watch, first the child discovers striking and depressing the pillow to be successful, then knocking the pillow aside, and finally picking up the pillow and setting it aside. He discovers that a pillow may be depressed, knocked aside, or set aside. Either striking or grasping is successful in removing the pillow to allow access to the watch. These subschemes are the beginning of construction of parameters of certain groups of objects' attributes. Certain objects may be depressed or lifted; others may not. Some such parameters are part of and define one object, but not another. Gradually the child eliminates these parameters as general constructs of objects. [All such parameters or attributes are parts of objects, which are distinct from objectness, and which begin to be separate in stage 6, but which are not completely separate until after the preconceptual stage (age two to four)]. He comes to understand that it is the edges' moving (relative to the self or to another object) as a set, more than the other parts of his activities, that determines his successful grasp of the watch. If someone else moves the object, that remains good enough to separate two objects. Under certain circumstances acting on the object with his eyes works as well as acting on the object with his hands.

The Factor of Edges

As stages continue, sets of edges finally become the most reliable visual criteria for objectness. Other parameters, depressibility or liftability, etc., are part of, or attributes of, specific objects. It is as if the system is a student of edges. Once the system is a scholar of edges, it has a self and object and other objects separate from one another.

Study of edges (acting on edges with the eyes) is probably a significant part of these behaviors, if not the critical factor that provides a biological base for cognitive development in stages 4 and 5. Construction of one object separate from another cannot rest on visual line/edge-gating exclusively, however, since it is likely that a congenitally blind child also constructs a world of separate objects. Nevertheless, one may readily see how a visual line/edge-movement gate functions like an embryological inductor, that when brought into play in a timely fashion it induces a shift in the organization of development. It is analogous to giving a worker or scientist a new tool. The organism must still interact with its environment to affect further development and production (as in stage 5), but the quality and speed of interaction may be shifted greatly. Viewing the line/edge-movement gate as an inductor in no way detracts from Piaget's view that the organism actively constructs his own world as the organism interacts with the social and physical environment.

Though hearing is not our focus, a few comments may be added. It is of interest that the neural tracts connecting the eye to the lateral geniculate body and those connecting the ear to the medial geniculate body are both fully myelinated at the same time, during the third or fourth month (Lecours, 1975). This precedes the beginning of stage 3, when the child's focus shifts from proximal aliment to distal aliment, that is, when his focus shifts to watching and listening. Rapid transmission from the eye or from the ear to the brain, that is, to the geniculate ganglia and, in some measure, to the cortex, would be enabling as the child centers on distal aliment, watching and listening.

Conclusions

In summary, Hubel and Weisel (1979) showed that the visual cortex may function as a line/edge-movement gating system. Lecours (1975) found that the optic tract connecting the retina to the visual cortex becomes fully myelinated at about six months and thus could be instrumental in bringing on-line a line/edge-movement gating system. This takes place just before stage 4 of the sensorimotor period begins. Such a gating system acts as an inductor supporting the change in mode of scheme organization in stages 4 and 5 relative to stages 2 and 3, and allowing the child to achieve a new equilibrium in stage 6 in which a scheme for one object may be distinguished from that for another.

NOTE

1. Using habituation measures, the tendency of one to lose interest when a stimulus is less novel, Kestenbaum, Termine, and Spelke's (Spelke, in Press) findings in three-month-olds support Piaget's position that initially two contiguous objects are not differentiated from each other.

Part II

A THEORY OF CONSCIOUSNESS

Chapter 4

PIAGET'S CONCEPTS REGARDING
CONSCIOUSNESS

Piaget's conceptualizations were always at the most general level. He referred to his object of study, the child, as the epistemic subject, the universal subject. He aimed at the broadest possible understanding of the psychology and biology of organisms. So it was with consciousness. He proposed understandings of consciousness at its most abstract and general level.

Cognition and Consciousness

Piaget (1973) viewed mental imagery as one form of thought and believed that thought was necessarily conscious, that it was meaningless to speak of unconscious thoughts or mental images, and that it was redundant to speak of conscious thought or conscious images. Piaget did not suggest that cognition was coincident with thought. Rather, he stressed that cognition, intelligent activity, mostly occurs outside of consciousness.

Piaget (1976) proposed that consciousness of intelligent activity develops from the "periphery" to the "center." (His terms periphery and center should not be confounded with peripheral and central nervous system.) In any particular behavior one is first aware of the goal and the results, both termed by Piaget the periphery. Gradually one becomes aware of how the object behaves as well as how the self behaves, both of which Piaget termed the center. For instance, a six-year-old child is able to push on the back of a ping-pong ball in such a way as to give it backspin, causing it to go forward and to return. The child knows what he wants the ball to do—his goal, the object's going forward and then returning. He also perceives the result, if the ball actually does so. He may be adept at the task long before he becomes aware of his own behavior, that he pushes on the back of the ball; or the object's behavior, that the ball spins backwards as it moves forward.

Like several authors before him, Piaget (1976) noted the alliance of unconscious intellectual processes with automatic function and the alliance of conscious processes with the novel. He, however, did not regard this as a sufficiently general conceptualization. He invoked his periphery-to-center concept. Thereby, awareness of disadaptation or of the novel, of a result failing to coincide with a wish or expectation, becomes only a special case of awareness of the periphery preceding awareness of the center.

Repression and Dominant Organization

Piaget (1973) proposed that in the intellectual domain a child represses or distorts knowledge that conflicts with his more dominant organization, that repression in the intellectual domain is much the same as in the emotional domain, where an impulse is repressed or distorted because it conflicts with a dominant superego concept. Freud's formulation regarding the dynamic unconscious and repression, and the lifting of repression, allowing consciousness, is a less general one than Piaget's. Piaget's concept embraces both the affective and intellectual domains, but also by invoking the concept of dominant organization it allows for repression of less primitive schemes by more primitive ones, not only the reverse.

Piaget (1973) reported examples of repression in the intellectual domain. For example, when a child first notices that the ping-pong ball with backspin on it is rotating backwards as it moves forward, he may comment on this backward rotation. Then, only a short time later, the child contradicts himself. In keeping with his usual understanding of movement of a ball, he now insists that the ball rotates forward as it moves forward. From behavior such as this Piaget concluded that the child repressed his new knowledge because it conflicted with his entrenched, dominant concept. Piaget (1976) also showed that the child may distort, not just repress his understanding, when such understanding conflicts with his dominant precept. For example, when a child learns to use a sling to throw a ball at a target, though adept at hitting the target, he may insist that he releases the ball at 12 o'clock, not at 9 o'clock where he actually releases it. This is in keeping with his understanding of what he does when he throws a ball which is not at the end of a sling. He faces the target and releases the ball directly in front of him at 12 o'clock. Over time, a child makes various distortions and compromises between his new observations of his activity or the object's activity and his dominant constructs. He may claim he released the ball at 6 o'clock or that the ball took a curved path. Finally, he states that in order to hit the target he released the sling when the ball was at 9 o'clock and that the ball followed the tangent of the circle made by the sling. So, either in the emotional or in the intellectual domain, repression or distortion or compromise takes place when one's understanding conflicts with one's dominant organization.

Consciousness and Logic

Piaget (1954) was unwilling to view consciousness as merely epiphenomenal. Yet he insisted that consciousness was neither substance nor energy. Consciousness could not be the "cause of a physiological phenomenon, nor of another state of consciousness" (p. 142). He stated that "consciousness is at the source of connections that depend on systems of meaning" (p. 142). In explicating the role of consciousness as one of implication or meaning, he focused on the development of awareness of logical necessity, a kind of consciousness first arising in the concrete operational period (eight to twelve years). For example, a concrete-operational child at one point realizes that if $2 + 2 = 4$, then $4 - 2$ must necessarily equal 2. This awareness of logical necessity is a new kind of awareness. Piaget stressed that $2 + 2$ does not cause 4 and that addition does not cause subtaction. These are not causal relationships. The essential relationship between states of consciousness is one of implication. That $2 + 2 = 4$ and that addition implies subtraction is a "relation of reason to consequence" (p. 142). He also showed how the role of consciousness is one of implication even in the less rigorous reasoning of the preoperational child (age two to seven). He stressed that the connection between conscious states is implication while the connection between physiological states is causal relationships. Logical necessity, mathematics, $2 + 2 = 4$, "are represented in states of consciousness which alone judge right or wrong in these connections" [although] "Maybe all mathematical operations could be explained causally in terms of neurological structures" (pgs. 142-143).

Piaget (1954) offered a precise but very general conceptualization of the relationship of the psychological to its biological substrate. He argued that the organization of conscious cognition must be isomorphic to some sort of underlying organization of neurophysiologic activity. By isomorphic he meant that there was a correspondence between the two systems, but less so than if the two systems were exactly parallel. He described the logical system that must underlie concrete operations and its isomorphic neurophysiologic network [i.e., addition $(A + A_1 = B)$, corresponding reverse operations $(B - A_1 = A)$, and operations of identity $(A - A_1 = 0)$] since awareness of logical necessity is the essence of concrete operations. He proposed that the logic of regulations[1] is isomorphic to the organization of the neurophysiologic network characteristic of the intuitive stage of the preoperational period and that the lattice and group, which are the underlying logics to formal operations, are isomorphic to the relations between neurophysiologic structures during adolescence. Piaget asserted that "the sense of logical necessity," this new consciousness which arises in the concrete operational period, is an outgrowth of discovery made as a consequence of the reorganization of cognitive structure which itself reflects an underlying reorganization of neurophysiologic (causally bound) relationships. Since the cognitive system now obeys certain "laws of composition (if $B = A + A_1$, then $B - A_1 = A$, etc.), 'awareness of necessity'" follows (p. 319).

Consciousness as an Emergent Phenomenon

Piaget implied that consciousness is emergent, a new discovery. A sense of conviction cannot be the significant part of this new awareness, since a sense of conviction is present in the preoperational child, who is unshakable in his belief that he has a longer stick if his stick extends beyond the end of another. So, the new acquisition is the sense of fit that derives from this system that embraces addition, subtraction, and identity. What is new is the awareness that all these things form a unit—that if you have one then you have the rest. The sense of necessity is constructed from recognition by the child that he is in a logic-tight system; whichever way he moves it all fits together. Piaget's concept of this sense of necessity also implies that if a concrete operational child were to add $2 + 2$ and get 5 instead of 4, then his neurophysiologic structures (which operate causally) would keep searching this (newly organized) relationship of structures. The search would continue because of the disequilibrium caused by the aliment 2-and-2-equals-5 being assimilated to existing structural relationships, an inherent part of which is the logic of necessity. At a different level of development, e.g., the preoperational period, or during sleep, the criteria for reaching closure would not be the same.

Piaget's concept of the role of consciousness is not greatly different from Sperry's (1981) more recently expressed view. Sperry spoke of consciousness as causal, but only in a special sense, that is, as a "supervening cause." He analogized that consciousness is like a wheel—the organization of molecules into a wheel is a supervening cause of the behavior of a wheel. The behavior of a wheel cannot be explained by the molecules of the wheel any more than the behavior of thought can be explained only by neurons or their biochemistry. Consciousness is an emergent property of the organization of the neuronal network and its biochemistry, but this emergent property has an overall governing effect on what will happen next in the total system. This effect cannot be explained on the biochemical or microscopic level, although the content of the biochemical and microscopic organization is employed in going from one thought to another. ". . . [C]onscious phenomena as emergent functional properties of brain processing exert an active control role as causal determinants in shaping the flow patterns of cerebral excitation" (p. 58). "Compared to the physiological processes, the conscious events are more molar being determined by configurational or organizational interrelations in neuronal functions. The mental entities transcend the physiological just as the physiological transcends the molecular, the molecular, the atomic and subatomic" (p. 58). He went on to write that his position is monistic, unlike Eccles's conscious self that survives death of the brain or Popper's unembodied "world 3," both parts of dualisms in which mental function has life of its own separate from the brain.

Piaget (1954, p. 143) drew a line between implication and causality when he proposed that implication is the "basic relationship between two states of consciousness, whereas physiological connections are characterized by causal relationships." There appears, nevertheless, to be little difference between Sperry's supervening causality and Piaget's implication. Piaget is more precise in not attributing causal force to consciousness per se. On the other hand, the structural relationship, part and parcel of the organization of conscious thought, and (according to Piaget) of the underlying neurophysiologic organizations, certainly has "supervening causal" effects. In the case of the child who is convinced that a ball can go forward only if it rolls forward, conscious conviction appears to have supervening causal influence on the underlying circuitry as he reverses his initial observation to conform to the dominant organization of his understanding of how balls move.

One distinction between Sperry's views and Piaget's is evident. In Piaget's conceptualization, while conscious cognition at a given level tends to conform to certain rules (most often those that are in keeping with the child's developmental level), unconscious cognition can at times also conform to those same high level rules, since unconscious cognition may also operate on the most sophisticated level of relationships between neurophysiologic organizations. Piaget does not explicitly make this point, but it follows from his concept. Accordingly, the relationship of implication or supervening cause, while it is the usual role of conscious cognition, is not the exclusive property of conscious cognition. Unconscious cognition also may operate in accord with high level implication, though it is not required to do so. The broader latitude of unconscious processes in choice of logic has been exemplified countless times in Freud's study of dreams, parapraxes, jokes, and symptoms. As already noted, a pun or a slip of the tongue, for instance, makes use of preconceptual thought process, similarities identifying two objects as the same and minor changes in an object defining it as a different object.

Development of Consciousness

As sketched in Chapter 2, Piaget traced the stepwise development of object schemes, beginning with a state in which schemes are very primitive, corresponding merely to reflex activities such as sucking or grasping. Starting with undifferentiated self-objects, in which the sucking or grasping scheme is all at once the object, the self, and the other object, Piaget charted the stages of transformation of such primitive schemes until the child's object schemes are separate from schemes of the self and separate from other object schemes.

Piaget's findings lend themselves to a similar stagewise differentiation of mental images, i.e., consciousness, starting with a state in which percept and mental image are undifferentiated from each other and culminating in a state in which percepts are distinct from mental images. In fact, Piaget's (1963, p. 327) comments that in stage 5 "representation is not yet freed from perception" and (p. 355) in stage 6 "images are liberated from direct perception and become 'symbolic'[sic]" would be in keeping with such a formulation. However, Piaget did not trace the development of mental images as stepwise differentiation of an undifferentiated percept-mental image. Instead, he viewed representational consciousness, mental imagery, as a phenomenon which emerges from a cognitive restructuring that takes place in stage 6 (eighteen months to two years), the final stage of the sensorimotor period. He contended that until stage 6 there is no persisting or evokable image (Piaget, 1954). The child's universe in stage 3 is only a totality of "pictures" emerging from nothingness at the moment of action to return to nothingness at the moment the action is finished (Piaget, 1954, p. 43). He stated that in stage 4 it was unnecessary that Jacqueline picture persons in their absence if she anticipated their coming through the door (Piaget, 1963, p. 252). In stage 5 search behind a single screen does not "presuppose that the subject imagines" [sic] the object under the screen, but simply . . . interprets the screen as a sign of the actual presence of the object" (1954, p. 84) which disappeared. Piaget (1973, p. 11) wrote that there is no thought prior to "symbolic evocation by speech, by mental pictures, and other means, which makes it possible to represent what the sensorimotor intelligence, on the contrary, is going to grasp directly."

While Piaget (1954, 1962a, 1963) used the word consciousness throughout his study of his children's sensorimotor cognition, he contended that consciousnesses were merely transient "pictures" that play little role in cognition during the first five stages of the sensorimotor period; that sensorimotor cognition and behavior are basically silent, i.e., unconscious, activities; that only after object permanence when there is "spacial *desubjectivation* and *consolidation*" (1954, p. 212) is there mental imagery integral to planning action. Any earlier "pictures" have no role in the construction of thought or conscious imagery; mental images are phenomena that emerge in stage 6 with no particular relationship to these earlier fleeting conscious "pictures."

Piaget (1962a) did not include these earlier pictures as part of his formulation of how a signifier is constructed. Rather, he proposed that the signifier portion of a mental image or symbol is constructed from interiorization of an action symbol. His formulation of development of a signifier rested heavily on an observation he made of his daughter Lucienne's behavior. In stage 4, wishing to obtain a chain from a partially open matchbox, she found herself stymied. While gazing at the box she opened her mouth wider and wider. She then used her finger to open the box further, enabling her to retrieve the chain. Through imitation of the box by opening her mouth she created a body-action symbol of the box's opening. Opening her mouth signified opening the box. Piaget assumed that later, when such imitative behavior was no longer manifest, her body action symbol or representation was interiorized,[2] was converted to (emerged as) a conscious mental image or thought. This unseen imitation was now the signifier part of the symbol.

Piaget (1962a) proposed that while imitation, almost pure accommodation, gives rise to the signifier part of the symbol, play, almost pure assimilation, provides the signified part of the symbol. Not until stage 6 is a child able to engage in make-believe (symbolic) play. In stage 6 Jacqueline (fifteen months) was able to make one object substitute for another when engaging in play. For example, since she generally fondled a pillow fringe when falling asleep, in stage 6 she pretended to fall asleep, as she fondled in place of the pillow fringe a cloth with fringe or the tail of her rubber donkey. The play, pretending to fall asleep, is that which is signified by the symbol, the fringy object assimilated to the pillow fringe scheme, which is part of the falling-asleep scheme. According to Piaget, in stage 6 when the two processes, assimilation and accommodation—play as the signified and imitation as the signifier—are reunited and covert, then mental image, representation or symbol, has been constructed.

Brown (1976, p. 73) stated, "Piaget has commented

that awareness in the young child begins not as an awareness of objects or an awareness of activity, but rather as an undifferentiated state out of which more highly developed levels emerge." In a general way one cannot argue with this conceptualization of Piaget's position. Piaget's position was that the form of a mental image is a construct made up of a specific amalgam of perception and action of the body symbol, an imitation of the object using the body which, after it is interiorized, may be active as a scheme without any overt action. To Piaget (Piaget & Inhelder, 1971) active imitation, motor action, is the essential mechanism in formation of a mental image symbol. It is interiorization of this motor action which joins or brings consciousness to cognition. Prior to stage 6 cognitive organization is just sensorimotor activity which may use but does not require consciousness. Consciousnesses are largely come-and-go, unattached phenomena which have no role in forming mental images.

In Piaget's developmental system there appear to be two major reorganizations in the development of cognition. One is from the sensorimotor period to the preoperational period. The second is from the preoperational period to the concrete operational period. Piaget posited interiorization of motor action as the basic transition mechanism involved in both these reorganizations. As summarized above, he proposed that interiorization of a body-action symbol reorganizes sensorimotor structures into representational, i.e. preoperational, structures. At the second major transition point in cognitive development, preoperational cognition is transformed into concrete operational cognition through interiorization of motor activity again. Piaget (Laurendeau & Pinard, 1970) suggested that the child's physically grouping like items together and then separating some of them (physically classifying objects), when interiorized, becomes mental classification or mental adding and subtracting. Both transitions are characterized by an adaptation to qualities of the object world without external activity, or interiorization.

Piaget's description of the interiorization of a body symbol in stage 6, giving rise to the form of a mental image, suggests that he was thinking of the mental image as if it were a whole object that is moved into the cognitive system and thereafter is much like a piece of furniture. It is for this reason that I think that Piaget, in spite of his pioneering constructivist emphasis, may have viewed thinking in a manner similar to Freud's, when Freud (1953) proposed that thinking is "an experimental way of acting." At least this seems so once representation is constructed in stage 6. In such a concept of thinking, it is as if thought consisted of moving objects around in one's mind, just as one might move furniture around in the physical world. Instead of walking to the refrigerator and opening the door to get some food, one moves one's self intrapsychically, crosses the room, opens the door, etc., the movement of the self and the door all taking place in one's mind rather than in the external world.

An Information Processing Model

In contrast with Freud's idea and in keeping with an information processing model, one may conceptualize intrapsychic movement of an object as an ordered array of changes that occur when an object moves in relationship to other objects, a sampling of the many interfaces or relationships between integrated sets of lines and colors, proprioceptive patternings, touching of this or that, and so forth. Piaget's constructivist approach lends itself to this latter kind of understanding of conscious and unconscious content: that the object and its activity are active by virtue of an array of definitions of relationships between this object and other objects, present and past. Granted the schemes will tend to be large-chunk schemes, but the chunk need not conform to whole object relative to other whole objects, a fully constituted self moving toward a fully constituted refrigerator, or the like.

The following examples give a flavor of the parameters or definitions out of which the child constructs his world. Many are parameters studied by Piaget, which are very complex interactions of simpler parameters. Some may primarily be derivatives of organic factors. One such parameter is the child's tracking of changes in interfaces between objects as one object passes by and obscures another. This obscuring of one object by another helps define space and objects. Reachability-graspability is another parameter. A further example would be a set of boundaries belonging to one object that moves as a set of lines when the object moves relative to a set of lines belonging to a relatively stationary object.[3] In time a child finds that objects fall, that if he lets go of an object or if he moves the object to the edge of a table, it probably will fall, and that he need not throw it to the floor (Piaget, 1963). He also finds that a round object that he sees roll will not necessarily do so without his giving it a push (Piaget, 1954). He learns that certain objects will fit into others and others will not, such as blocks in a bucket, that they must have a certain matching of shapes (Piaget, 1954).

In time the child learns that an object will not pass through another object, that objects have boundaries.[4] This is another fundamental, but complex defining parameter of objectness, not just a parameter of a specific object. In our gravitational setting one object lies on top of another object, obscuring it from above.[5] Another parameter of an object is that if it disappears behind a cushion, it is likely to be under the cushion. Later, it will become evident that one of the fundamental distinctions between a perceptual scheme and an ideational or mental image scheme is whether the scheme was aroused last by external aliment, whether it was an ultimate or penultimate activity. Thus, sequencing of schemes helps define a type of image.

These parameters of activities, sequencing of schemes, movement of edges of schemes, incomplete edges of schemes, of schemes being further to reach, and so on, all are integrations of many varied experiences. They integrate countless organized patterns of stimulation and still more individual stimuli. Assimilations tend to employ large chunks to find the right relationship in order to understand or to retrieve information. A particular relationship, however, may rest on one or several small factors. For example, if an object has a slight irregularity instead of a smooth curve to its edge, the child may pull the object by its extension—its irregularity. While large-chunk assimilation is the trend, small differentiations may be a part of the identification of a particular object or activity. There is no absolute boundary or clear ordering in the search of the systems of schemes. On introspection, each of us can find examples of search of our system similar to the one offered by Piaget (1963, p. 345). In a rush when driving his car, Piaget used his handkerchief to wipe some oil from his steering wheel. Rather than soil his pocket, he wedged the rag deeply into the crevice between two seats. The device to hold the windshield open being defective, he could only shut it or leave it completely open. It was too warm to shut it and too rainy to leave it open. Fatigued from holding it open with his hand, he was unable to find an object to prop the windshield open. He noted the angle between the windshield and an upright of the car body. Having a notion of the analogy of the angle as a solution, he found himself automatically reaching for the handkerchief. The automatic going from wedge shape to wedge shape is a relatively large-chunk based search, but it is also far from looking for a fully constructed object, the handkerchief, or a picture of the whole self placing something between the fully pictured windshield and car upright. One may only assume that many other possible unconscious solutions were also attempted at the same time, having to do with transparencies of windows, with rain and getting out of the rain, etc., until the correct match took place.

This constructivist or reconstructivist approach does not lend itself to viewing a mental image of an object as if it were a piece of furniture that is moved around. The mental image as furniture is especially inappropriate when one considers that such phenomena as the obscuring of one object by another and the inability of one object to pass through another are the result of countless coordinations of visual sensorimotor schemes acting on different sets of edges and with tactile sensorimotor schemes, acting on the same object or different ones of different shape and weight in different settings, coordinating observations as to how these parameters change or do not change with rotation, etc. which must be held separate in some sort of coordination. An object in motion becomes a very long potential list or program with many aggregations and abbreviating bypasses, some data processed in parallel, some processed serially. Even with aggregations and shortcuts, the list is very long, but then such a program has a very long history, when we consider the almost constant exploration and practice engaged in by an extremely active organism, the child. As formidable as is the number of observations made by Piaget of his children, it constitutes but a small fraction of their activities as they explored themselves and their world. I am ready to believe the anecdote that an adult athlete, in top condition, attempting to imitate a child's every move, shortly became exhausted.

An object-in-motion as a construct is analogous to interference patterns or to algorithms (of information processing). Thinking (or perception) of a block moving from A to B is not moving the image of a block intrapsychically, but is a sampling of a large number of changes in the aliment for the scheme of the block relative to the scheme of its setting, were the block to move from A to B. If the block were to move from A to B, some of the parameters of schemes for the block would be rewritten, including changes related to the transition period, until the block arrived at B. It is not the movement of an image, but an algorithm (probably incomplete and yet redundant) for the many changes in relationship that occur if, or as, the block moves. In thought, it is only as if one were moving objects around. The view of thinking as the moving around of images of objects as if images were furniture is a construction, as is an object or an attribute. At one point a child has the know-how that defines solid objects as images which may not pass through each other, but may rest upon one another, may be further to reach than an object that partially precludes seeing them, and so forth. But even that will be processed potentially as wedge-shaped or round, seen or felt, blue or red, maleable or rigid, reachable, swingable, etc. Once there is representation we do not consider any of these parameters as, for example, we write using a pen. But when we do consciously think about our activity, the pen is not a complete object unless we make a special effort. Rather, it is some combination of the pressure against the finger and part of the color or point and the writing coming out. Yet, all the other parameters are potential and could be brought together in a construct of the pen as a visual object or tactile object and the writing as motor behavior.

Presumably unconscious construction includes more particulate and widespread parameters, but even less coherent pictures of one object or one activity.

Piaget and the Genetics and Dynamics of Consciousness

Piaget addressed both the genetics (development) and the dynamics of consciousness. He clarified two general laws of the dynamics of consciousness. First, consciousness in both the socio-emotional and intellectual domains tends to conform to the dominant organization of the schemes. If an understanding fails to fit the dominant organization, it likely will be ignored, repressed, or distorted. Repression in accord with superego demands becomes only a special case of an understanding being excluded from consciousness because it does not conform to the dominant organization, in this case the dominant organization being the superego. Second, consciousness develops from the periphery to the center, the periphery being goals and results, the center being behavior of the self and behavior of the object. Then disadaptation or the novel being conscious is merely one example of awareness starting at the periphery, that is, failure of result to match expectation or wish. In these two formulations of the dynamics of consciousness, Piaget provided us with very general rules governing what will be conscious in a given instance.

Piaget's formulation of the genetics of consciousness taken from "Problem of Consciousness" (1954) along with his more commonly known presentation in *Play, Dreams and Imitation in Childhood* (1962a), essentially has consciousness, mental imagery, deriving from structure or restructuring. This is almost parallel to Freud's concept of consciousness arising from energy—hypercathexis—a kind of internal combustion. Both seem to treat thought or consciousness as if it were a kind of energy. (In Piaget's formulation, interiorization turns the light on imitation.)

In the ensuing chapters, I propose a theory of development of consciousness not greatly different in basic form from Piaget's construction of objects and attributes of objects. Just as the child builds himself and the object world, so he builds a more refined consciousness out of his waking state.

NOTES

1. The logic of regulations is a one-way logic, typical of the intuitive stage (five to seven) child. If he looks at a set of moun-

tains, he cannot imagine that his view would change were he to change his vantage point (Piaget, 1937).

2. Interiorization is not to be confused with internalization, incorporation into the self representation. If interiorization of imitation were the primary transition mechanism, as assumed by Piaget, then it would be by interiorization in stage 6 that both self representation and object representations would be constructed. Later, after self and object representations are formed, then interiorization would include either internalization, that is incorporation into the self representation, or incorporation into an object representation.

3. This example of course refers to Chapter 3.

4. In no sense should it be thought that the child has a conscious concept that the fundamental defining characteristic of an object is its boundaries. Instead, he has the know-how that objects are sets of boundaries that move together and that do not penetrate other sets of boundaries.

5. These parameters are a function of the (gravitational) setting, and of having a sensory apparatus that responds to electromagnetic radiation of a restricted range—visible light. These parameters would not hold for constructing objectness if we were raised in a gravitationless setting, or if we had an infrared sensor rather than a light sensor.

Chapter 5

CONSCIOUSNESS IN THE FIRST HALF
OF THE SENSORIMOTOR PERIOD
(0–8 mo.)

In Piaget's concept of the development of consciousness, consciousness was derived from reorganization of structure. The mental image was formed by interiorization of a body action, Lucienne's opening her mouth (1962a). He also had awareness of logical necessity, a new understanding, deriving from the restructuring of the schemes that takes place in the concrete operational period (1954).

The position I take does not agree with the concept that consciousness is some special property of the central nervous system or with Piaget's (1962a, and 1954) or Sperry's (1981) inference that consciousness somehow emerges from the complexity of organization of the central nervous system.

Piaget's observations and some of his theoretical concepts provide the structure for building an understanding of differentiation of mental image. His digestive model not only maintains the analogy of the nervous system function to that of other biologic systems, but also captures the spirit of the interaction of the psychologic being with its world, even though the basis for such overall function appears (as already suggested in Chapter 2) to be reducible to the organization of particulate input and output, now that we have learned more about the differential wiring and chemistry of the nervous system.

Piaget's Sensorimotor Scheme

Of most importance to the argument that follows is Piaget's concept of the scheme, a holistic configuration of activity in the central nervous system, which sustains and develops itself by assimilating aliment; namely patterns of sensorimotor stimulation. As mentioned in Chapter 2, given the scheme's basic tendency to assimilate the largest chunks of aliment that have temporal coincidence or configurational resemblance to it, a scheme assimilates much aliment that, to an outside observer, is irrelevant or coincidental. For example, aliment corresponding to warmth of the room or to position of the body may be part of the sucking scheme, provided such aliment is frequently part of the sucking situation. Since many of the coincidental nutrients will not be repeated regularly enough to be included, they will drop away or be overlapped by other nutrients. Of course, such aliment, relevant or irrelevant, will be assimilated at the level of the scheme's organization; if an infant sucks a toy train, his sucking scheme includes the hardness and shape of the train, but ignores such features as that it may be rolled on the floor or that it may be the focus of a make-believe game.

The position I take regarding the development of consciousness is that, to begin with, consciousness is coincident with wakefulness and that essentially only one waking—that is, only one conscious—scheme may be active at any one time. Initially any simultaneous scheme activity is a part of any other ongoing activity. Later, taking into account maturation as the developing organism interacts with the environment, schemes become reorganized. Hence, the conscious schemes or subschemes are also reorganized.

In the early stages, a sensorimotor scheme is largely undifferentiated. For example, the sucking is both the self and the object as well as being constituted by components which have little to do with sucking or feeding. Both motor and sensory activity involving sucking are this same scheme. Motor activity, such as turning the head toward the mother's breast, satiation, and even failure to be satiated are not separate from each other and are part of the sucking scheme of the newborn child. A visual scheme for an object is as much aliment coming from the proprioceptive tracts, stimuli coming from eye muscles and neck muscles (or any intracranial feedback of motor neuron activity) when the child tracks the object, as it is stimuli taking origin in the retina. Looking at any object becomes acting on it with the eyes and neck as well.

The scheme of an object is an undifferentiated amalgam of all of these sources. As undifferentiated as are these schemes of the object to begin with, they are the object to the child. They are that out of which the child will construct his objects, including the self. To the newborn, the sucking scheme with all its components is the breast and is the self.

If all these components including coincidental ones are part of the scheme, then it follows that *no scheme is the property of any one type of aliment.* Accordingly, although the sucking scheme is generally aroused by stimulation of the lips, if sense of pleasure, warmth from an adjacent body, movement of one's head toward the warmth, movement of one's mouth, lips, and tongue, and one's usual body position are also integral to the sucking scheme, then it is expectable that the breast need not always be present to activate (to be assimilated by) the sucking scheme, that one or several of the other types of aliment may also activate the sucking scheme. The sucking scheme may arise from combinations of hunger, satiation, warmth, a familiar position, etc. The sucking scheme activity aroused by stimuli coincidental to feeding at the breast is somewhat, though not significantly, different from the configurations aroused in the presence of the breast, just as the particular sucking scheme activity varies somewhat as it accommodates to different nipples and body positions. In whatever manner such scheme activity is activated and whether it is covert or not, that is; whether the child is seen to suck or not, when the sucking scheme is activated, it is basically the same configuration of activity.

That a scheme is not the property of any one type of aliment allows for constructing a "picture" of an object in the absence of that object. For example, the breast-sucking scheme may be active in the absence of the breast. In my view, this early undifferentiated picturing of an object, this spectacle, is a type of hallucinatory phenomenon. The role of hallucination in thought formation was integral to Freud's theory of the development of thought as it is to the thesis I present in Chapter 6, although there is considerable difference between the two theories.

Beginning with fully undifferentiated and primitive schemes corresponding to aspects of reflex behavior in stage 1, Piaget (1963), 1962a, 1954) charted stagewise behavior changes until he could infer from the child's behavior in stage 6 that the schemes corresponding to different objects are distinct from each other. Piaget was also able to infer that the stage-6 child has mental representations or mental images.

Another Perspective on Consciousness

Piaget did not propose—as I will—that percept and mental image differentiate simultaneously out of a com-

mon anlage. He also outright resisted the idea of a perceptual origin to mental images (Piaget & Inhelder, 1971, p.
367). As described in Chapter 4, he instead had percepts
formed in stage 5 (Piaget, 1954), to be followed in stage 6
by the formation of mental images constructed out of interiorization of imitation. Hence, Piaget's position was that
consciousness is an emergent phenomenon, in that consciousness arises from the complexity of reorganization that takes place during a particular stage of development.

Why Piaget, in theorizing how images are constructed, did not propose a path parallel to his theory
of object construction (as I do) is not clear. Perhaps Lucienne's imitating of the opening of the matchbox had a
compelling influence on him. Perhaps the major influence
was his investment in the importance of motor activity in
learning about the world and in constructing images. Perhaps it was the observation that action, know-how, often
precedes mentation, knowing. It seems most likely that
Piaget's reason for proposing mental imagery as an emergent construct of stage 6 was his concern that the representative nature of mental imagery be accounted for.
However, the mental image or symbol in stage 6 or in the
preconceptual stage generally is not representative in the
sense of being separate from what it represents. Signifier
is not fully differentiated from signified. Make-believe
play is not make-believe to the two- to four-year-old. If a
two- to four-year-old wears a badge he is the sheriff. Also,
the word and the thing it stands for are not differentiated
from each other. When Jacqueline (two years) wanted a
garment from a cold room, she needed only to announce
that it was not cold in order to make the room not cold for
her (Piaget, 1962a). The room, the words "not cold"—
soon to be symbolic—and the attribute of coldness-not
coldness are just part-objects with no clear separation from
each other.

The Biology of Consciousness

My position is that consciousness is simply the awake stage of the sleep-wake cycle. A few remarks about the biology of consciousness—wakefulness—may help the reader understand the matrix into which I would fit my concepts. Awake to asleep, consciousness to unconsciousness, is a series of stages in which the brain is more to less responsive to or activated by sensory input and in which the brain has more to less access to motor activity. Presumably these stages are largely under neurophysiologic control, although all points between psychologic control and physiologic control exist.

One may stay awake, though sleepy, and one may, to some extent, will oneself to sleep. Some people fall asleep when overwhelmed with feelings. Others are unable to sleep when emotionally stimulated. Still others fall asleep when hungry. The sleep state is highly selective. For example, when asleep a mother may respond to her infant's cry, while a father responds to the telephone's ring. So there is a complex interplay of psychologic and physiologic factors involved in control of sleep, but generally and ultimately the sleep-wake cycle is under physiologic control

In recent years the roles of the ascending reticular activating system in sustaining wakefulness and the raphe nuclei in sustaining or inducing sleep have been discovered (Kaplan, Freedman, & Sadock, 1980). It is unclear whether sleep is absence of wakefulness or wakefulness is absence of sleep. Each state is a yield of an interaction. Nonetheless, ability to have a waking state is the norm, prolonged unconsciousness generally is coincident with damage or death (although in rare conditions sustained wakefulness occurs when the raphe nuclei are damaged).

One might assert that consciousness is the intact connectedness of the central nervous system to the peripheral nervous system enhanced by the ascending reticular activating system and dampened by the raphe nuclei. The sleep-wake cycle ranges in stages from deep sleep through light sleep to waking and finally to alertness, or even to a state of hyperalertness. Although a newborn may be more or less awake, more or less conscious, he is not in any way self-aware, conscious of the self. To be self-aware a child must have relatively advanced structuring. He must develop constructs of self and objects. He must have some awareness of outside, some "looking" at things, hence, some sense of the self "looking" at things. In keeping with Piaget's (1976) stages of cognitive development, the sense of self sensing things is not complete until the concrete operational period (eight to eleven years), and develops still further during the formal operational period (twelve to eighteen years) when the adolescent senses his own sensing processes, that is, when he thinks about his thinking.

None of these organizations is available to the newborn. Yet, in order to develop these organizations, only a few classes of built-in structures are essential. Only neurophysiologic underpinnings of the sleep-wake cycle, the reflex schemes and affects need to be taken as given. Built-in central nervous system configurations of potential stimulation corresponding to exercise of different reflexes (such as sucking versus extensor reflexes) or configurations corresponding to different affects (for instance, satiation or hunger versus startle response) necessarily constrain, a priori, any absolute undifferentiation of the newborn's schemes. Other biological constraints on undifferentiation, or structurings, develop as the central nervous system matures. For example, increased myelination of fibers serving particular brain centers necessarily shape neurophysiologic organization, hence, psychologic organization. In chapter 3, one such relationship between brain maturation and psychologic function was addressed in detail. Although it is likely that other major neurophysiologic factors are yet to be discovered and that they will have their impact on understanding psychologic function, it is unnecessary to invoke any classes of innate structures other than these already known types in order to outline a theory of mental imagery.

Waking Schemes Are Consciousness

In the theory to be presented I contend that, after stage 1 (0–1 month) of the sensorimotor period, all schemes inferred (by Piaget) from observation of stage-typical behavior are waking schemes. That is, all such schemes occur during the waking phase of the sleep-wake cycle. I also contend that such schemes fill and constitute consciousness. The waking phase is viewed merely as a state of enhanced connectedness of the central and peripheral nervous system. The flux of enhanced connectedness is a function of developmental and current dynamic psychologic factors, plus physiologic factors, and is part of the activity of every scheme that is inferred from observation of stage-typical behavior in the sensorimotor period. (The rules for psychologic factors outlined by Piaget were presented above, pages 82–83.) As the fluctuating stimulation which originates in retinal cones sensitive to red light is part of schemes out of which redness, in contrast to greenness, is eventually constructed, so the fluctuating stimulation related to an overall connectedness of central nervous system schemes to the peripheral nervous system is a part of schemes out of which percepts and mental images are eventually constructed. (Affect, another major class of conscious content, will be addressed in Chapter 7.)

Piaget stresses that in the newborn we find no evidence that schemes are differentiated into objects, percepts, or mental images. In stage 1, the child merely practices his reflexes. For example, he becomes better at sucking when his mouth is stimulated and better at grasping when his palm is stimulated. His schemes in the central nervous system merely correspond to this reflex behavior.

Basically, this same level of undifferentiation continues through stage 3 (eight to twelve months). When Jacqueline made certain movements including her foot striking a doll attached to the crib, thus causing the doll to bounce, to her the scheme of watching the doll bounce was not separate from her movements, since when Piaget (1963, p. 160) held the doll out of contact with the crib or the foot, she still went through her movements on seeing the doll. The visual scheme of the doll moving is assimilated to the motor and sensory scheme of her movements and vice versa. All are part of one interconnected, patterned activity in the nervous system. When Piaget (1963, p. 201) drummed on a tin box and then stopped, Laurent went through his repertoire to make interesting spectacles last. He shook his arm, drew himself up, struck his coverlets, and so on, while looking at the tin box. He did this a number of times over a period of a month. The listening scheme is assimilated to the movement schemes and vice versa. The subschemes of the drumming noise and the movements are part of one scheme. *In stage 3 as in stage 2 every configuration of activity taking place within the same time frame is part of one big scheme. Only one waking scheme may be active at any one time since additional aliment is either assimilated to the scheme that is active or replaces it as the active scheme.*[1]

Circular Reactions Are Conscious

For my argument it is particularly important that stage 2 and 3 schemes, primary and secondary circular reactions, largely occur in the awake, that is, conscious, state. Some repetitive behavior, such as sucking, certainly takes place during sleep, but circular reactions apparently do not. Even if an example of a primary or secondary circular reaction during sleep could be documented, clearly nothing approaching the frequency and variety of primary or secondary circular reactions is manifest by the sleeping child compared to the awake child. While asleep, a child does not repeatedly grasp and let go or repeatedly strike while watching or strike while listening.

What is conscious in the first three stages? As noted earlier, consciousness initially is merely wakefulness, a phase of the sleep-wake cycle when the central and the peripheral nervous systems are in better contact with each other. The waking state is a state of the nervous system when stimulation of the specific sensory (touch, taste, visual) neurons is likely to impact the brain and when stimulation within the brain is likely to impact the voluntary muscles. Thus wakefulness or consciousness is reduced to a mechanical phenomenon, a phase in the sleep-wake cycle when connectedness between the brain and the peripheral nervous system is enhanced.[2]

In the first month, stage 1, little may be said about the relationship between scheme activity and the waking state, or consciousness, since awake or asleep the child sucks when his lips are stimulated and grasps when his palm is stimulated. His grasping or sucking schemes may be active awake or asleep.

In the early part of stage 2, however, a change takes place. At about eight weeks of age, grasping and sucking reflexes may be elicited when the child is asleep, but no longer when he is awake (Vaughn & McKay, 1975). Apparently in stage 2 reflex schemes are inhibited during wakefulness, while, as noted, circular reactions, activities which characterize stages 2 and 3, occur primarily, if not exclusively, in the waking state.

Two points are to be made here. First, beginning in stage 2, schemes that are active in the awake or conscious state are divided from schemes that are active in the sleeping or unconscious state. At least during early stage 2, more primitive schemes—reflex schemes—are active during unconsciousness. Also, as noted on page 93, stage 2- and 3-typical schemes, the circular reactions, are active during consciousness. Hence, any scheme inferred from circular reaction behaviors has, as part of it, an enhanced connectedness of the brain to the peripheral nervous system.

If the scheme inferred from stage-typical behavior occurs only in the waking state and if, as already noted, a scheme that is active assimilates all aliment which is active at the same time and ignores what it cannot assimilate, only one waking scheme may be active at one time. Put another way, *the active waking scheme that is inferred from stage-typical behavior in stages 2 and 3 necessarily fills or is coincident with consciousness.* Any scheme in stage 2 or 3 revealed by its behavioral components is to a significant degree connected to the peripheral nervous system. The anlage for consciousness of self and objects in this system is this particular configuration of activity in the nervous system, a state of connectedness of the brain to the peripheral nervous system.

Subschemes and Abbreviated Schemes

That the waking scheme of stage 2 or 3 fills or is consciousness does not imply that all subschemes of a circular reaction are conscious. It does not stipulate which subschemes of an active waking scheme are unconscious to begin with or become so, which subschemes get lost as the primary scheme develops; or how physiologic or psychologic constraints alter the form taken by a scheme. That the waking schemes of stages 2 and 3 constitute consciousness does not even mean that a child's stage-typical scheme may be active only when he is awake, when he is conscious; or that a stage-typical scheme, if active, must show behavioral components. Finally, the fact that waking schemes of stage 2 and 3 constitute consciousness does not dictate the waking scheme's structure, which, consistent with Piaget's (1973) work, tends to conform to the level of differentiation of manifest waking schemes, that is, would tend to keep pace with development.

Consider the proposition that even though a currently active scheme fills consciousness, not all parts of it must be active or conscious every time the scheme is manifest in behavior. Waking schemes often are abbreviated. As mentioned in Chapter 2, a stage-3 child who has repeatedly struck an object, causing it to swing, may imitate the swinging of that object by swinging his hand or may imitate his own past striking movement with an abbreviated striking movement (Piaget, 1962a). In such instances we may not detail precisely which parts of his usual strike-and-swing-the-object scheme are not active, but we may be certain that since part of the scheme is not expressed, part of it is not active.

In stage 3, when a child is reaching for an object, if one casts a kerchief over the object, the child interrupts his reaching unless his hand grazes the object, or unless he is already making a grasping movement. The child may cry, indicating continued interest in the object (scheme). He may look to the hand of the experimenter who put the object under the screen. To the child, the experimenter's hand scheme is part of the object scheme. Piaget (1954) noted that in none of these cases did the child reach behind the screen or attempt to remove the screen. Piaget spoke of the picture entering the void. It seems more likely that the picture scheme, an image scheme of some form, is still active when the child cries, or when he looks at the experimenter's hand, although the picture may be very undifferentiated. We have only very limited knowledge of what form the image takes. In the case of the child's looking at the experimenter's hand, the image certainly has a visual component and, in the case of the child's hand having to be making a grasping movement or having had to graze the object, his image certainly has proprioceptive or motor components and a sensation of touch respectively, and perhaps no visual component at all.

If a child causes a mobile to swing by striking it with his hand, he may next use arching of his body, producing the same effect; at another time he may stay exclusively with one action or the other. Also, the visual object he acts upon may differ (it may be a doll) at different times. He may vary the vigor of his motor action as he watches the activity of the mobile. In all these variations presumably the same global scheme is active, while some subscheme relationships are stable in some instances, vary in other instances, and are covert in still other instances.

The Scheme Is Probabilistic

The point is that a scheme is a probabilistic configuration, that when we infer that a scheme is active we cannot fully predict which subschemes are active and which are not. We only know that the entire scheme and its component subschemes are potentially more active than subschemes which are related to another scheme. This becomes important in Chapter 8 when we emphasize that a scheme, each time a reconstruction, is a potential configuration, not fully set in its location or in its constituent parts or their interrelationships.

To sum up at this point, Piaget argued that mental image is a construct of stage 6, the mechanism being interiorization of imitative action. His formulation assumes the mental image has no special relationship to earlier forms of consciousness and that mental image is the yield of transformation of structure, interiorization of imitative action. I propose that consciousness is present all along as a state of the sleep-wake cycle. While the cognitive organizations in stage 1, such as sucking schemes, are indistinguishable awake or asleep, beginning in stage 2 schemes whose forms correspond to stage-typical behavior are somewhat separate from unconscious schemes, although they are not separate from each other. As undifferentiated as they are, these schemes, typical for stage 2 or 3, are conscious, that is, they have enhanced connections to the peripheral nervous system. To begin with, such images are no more representative in the sense of being-in-place-of than they are separate from percepts or than one object scheme is separate from another. Yet, the organization of these images changes as a function of development and as a function of the rules that govern consciousness.

If a stage 2 or 3 scheme is inferred from behavior, it is a waking scheme. If simultaneously active waking schemes are limited in number, probably limited to one during the first three stages, and if a scheme assimilates ongoing (CNS) activity at the scheme's level of organization (though particular aliment may be only coincidental aliment) while bypassing an activity which is too out of keeping with the scheme's level of organization, then such *waking schemes fill, or are, consciousness*. Finally, integral to these waking schemes is the flux in the sleep-wake cycle out of which will be constructed a sense of consciousness, including vividness of an object and awareness of the self. This construction is no different from activity in a set of cones of the retina, which is sensitive to red light, being the anlage for construction of the attribute of redness, while activity in another set of cones is the anlage for blueness.

NOTES

1. It is possible that two schemes, for instance sucking and kicking, might be simultaneously active and completely separate; that is, have no relationship to one another. Consciousness would be completely divided. It would be as if one of the

schemes occurred at a different time. If they have a relationship, however, the relationship is that of one (sub)scheme assimilated to the other. They are part of only one active scheme. In stage 3 or before there is no evidence of any coordination between the schemes that demonstrates a distinction of one simultaneously active scheme from another.

2. Since certain motor and sensory systems are not myelinated, hence not in operation, until sometime after birth, it is apparent that such a maturational change will affect the amount and modalities of connectedness of brain with periphery.

Chapter 6

CONSCIOUSNESS IN THE SECOND HALF OF THE SENSORIMOTOR PERIOD (8–24 mo.)

Having described the global form of conscious schemes inferred from behavior in the first 3 stages, I will describe behaviors in the next 3 stages, which allow us to infer the forms conscious schemes take as they become increasingly differentiated from each other. While in the first 3 stages a cumulative developmental mode is primary, in the second 3 stages a differentiating developmental mode is primary.

The Arising of Differentiation

Prior to stage 4, as was stressed, simultaneously active schemes are not differentiated from each other. Beginning with stage 4, certain behavior allows us to infer that one scheme is distinct along certain parameters from another scheme that is active in the same time frame. In stage 4, when a pillow is between the child and watch, a child becomes adept, in steps, at removing the pillow in order to grasp the watch (Piaget, 1963). First he may strike the pillow, knocking it aside. Later, he may pick it up and set it aside. We may infer that to some extent he differentiates the pillow from the watch, that is, one object scheme is differentiated from another, since he behaves differently toward the two objects, removing the pillow and retrieving the watch. At the same time his scheme of the self is partially separate from his scheme of an object as evidenced by intent or preference. Also a scheme of part of the self is somewhat separate from another part of the self, as is evidenced by his striking or setting aside behavior taking place before he grasps.

In Chapters 2 and 3 the limits of such differentiation of one object scheme from another have been presented in some detail (not only for stage 4, but also for stage 5). Recall that a stage-4 child will not reach for a matchbox resting on a book (Piaget, 1954). He may reach for the book instead. Apparently the scheme of the matchbox and the scheme of the book merge. Only if the matchbox slides on the book will the child reach for the matchbox. For a child to distinguish one object from another without their moving relative to each other, the overlap of their boundaries must be minimal as in the example of the goblet resting on the book.

In stage 5 distinctions between object schemes become more refined. A child differentiates the box scheme from the cushion (upon which it rests) scheme without the box having to move relative to the cushion. The box being too far to reach, he will pull the cushion to him and then grasp the box (Piaget, 1963). In order to distinguish one object scheme from the other he no longer relies upon the movement of the boundaries between two objects that overlap, or upon the boundaries being separate as in the cushion and the watch, or upon the overlap of boundaries being minimal, as in the case of the goblet on the book. In stage 5 he will even pull on a string attached to an object in order to retrieve it. Not only is he not fooled by an overlap, he capitalizes on the small overlap of boundaries, recognizing that even a small connection (the string) to an object is an extension of that object (Piaget, 1963). So we have these major gains in the articulated differentiations of one object scheme and another. One may infer that in stage 5 a percept scheme is generally separate from another simultaneously active percept scheme, since he picks up an object resting on its platform and pulls on an extension of an object in order to retrieve it.

What about percept schemes and mental image schemes? Are they differentiated from each other in stages 4 and 5? As already detailed, in stage 4 a child will search for an object most regularly under a screen where he last successfully found that object (Piaget, 1954). One may view his scheme of the object-being-hidden, a very recent percept, as undifferentiated from his mental image or memory scheme of where it was found before. Since the object itself is not visible, it cannot be considered to be merely a percept. It's scheme must be a mental image.

It should be understood that Piaget would not agree that this scheme of where it was found before is a mental image. To Piaget, it it just an unconscious scheme that was part of the screen where he had found it before (not to be denied) and that had a high potential for being active and could be expressed behaviorally. In my view it is a scheme, part of which is conscious, although it is certainly not representative, either in the sense that an image stands in place of the real thing, or in the sense that an image and the thing it represents are distinct from each other. To be representative requires mental image to be distinct from percept (the real thing).

What about percept and mental image in stage 5? Are they still indistinct from each other? If an object is placed in the experimenter's hand, a first screen, then if the experimenter's fist enclosing the object is passed under a cushion, a second screen, and the object left under the cushion, the stage-5 child will usually search in the experimenter's hand, but not under the cushion. It appears that the child's mental image of the watch is not distinct from his percept of the watch going into the hand.

So, in stages 4 and 5 percept and mental image are not distinct from each other. Are percept and mental image conscious? Schemes inferred from stage-typical behavior of stages 4 and 5 (like those of 2 and 3) appear to be waking, that is, conscious schemes. An unconscious child could not be expected to evidence the typical motivated behaviors of these stages, such as knocking a pillow aside or searching behind a screen in order to reach a watch, or making increasingly refined distinctions between objects. A stage-5 child studies an object as he rotates it and brings it closer to or further from his eyes (Piaget, 1954). He watches the trajectory of objects as he drops them. He fills and empties containers. After inadvertently flipping an object by pressing on its edge, he experiments, pressing on it in various locations until he rediscovers and is able to do deliberately what he did by chance. These types of purposeful behaviors, so dependent on observation by the child, appear to demand consciousness.

Finally, in stage 6, in the circumstance when a child searches for the watch not just in the experimenter's hand, but also under the cushion, a second screen (Piaget, 1954) not only is the watch scheme distinct from the other object schemes, the two screens, but it is also distinct from the self scheme, although, as has been pointed out, even as late as the preconceptual stage, object schemes are not always distinct from one another. Nevertheless, when the child searches under the cushion when all he saw was the watch disappearing into the hand and the hand passing under the cushion, he must have a mental image of the watch which is distinct from his percept of the watch going into the hand (or from the cushion). In stage 6 conscious schemes, that is, mental representations, are undoubtedly necessary in order to explain certain behaviors, such as search for an object behind a second screen or delayed imitation, in which a child engages in behavior which she has never exhibited before, but which she witnessed recently (Piaget, 1962a, p. 63).

Simultaneous Schemes

In Chapter 5 we concluded that prior to stage 4 a stage-typical scheme fills consciousness. In stages 4 to 6 this is no longer necessarily true. No longer is one scheme either replaced by another or absorbed as a part of it, assimilated into it. The stage-typical schemes are conscious, but take a different form. Schemes may be active side by side, processed as distinct in some measure, based on the coordination of relationships between them. In another sense simultaneously active schemes are not separate since the very parameters that separate the schemes also bind them together by coordinating them in specific relationships. After stage 3, and especially in stage 6, when we see stage-typical behavior we may be certain that at times mental image subschemes which are distinct from that behavior are also active but covert. By stage 6, a whole[1] scheme of an object may be active without a behavioral component of it showing, as is implied by a child's having an autonomous mental image when searching behind a second screen.

It is unlikely that stage-typical behavior takes place without part of the scheme corresponding to that behavior being conscious. That stage-typical behavior indicates that at least parts of the underlying scheme are conscious is supported by the scheme's tendency to assimilate what it can at the level it can. Stage-typical behavior corresponds to schemes that are sufficiently novel and yet integral to a dominant focus, thereby meeting two of Piaget's (1976, 1973) qualifications for conscious cognition.

Before we become content with the concept that mental image is autonomous when the child searches behind a

second screen, let us ask a question. Is not a percept sup-
posed to be conscious, current (in his perceptual field at
the moment), and dependent on the object's presence;
while mental image is conscious, may or may not be current, but is not dependent on presence of the object? If
this is the case, search behind a second screen for a watch
does not necessarily indicate that the mental image of the
watch and the percept of the watch are completely separate. The child is not both looking at the watch and at the
same time having a mental image of a watch while the two
images are distinct from each other. It is more accurate to
say that mental image and percept are processed as separate, since the percept of the watch going behind the first
screen is also a memory or mental image, not a percept,
once the watch is out of sight. In a sense the child is processing as separate two mental images, one of which was a
percept a very short time ago.

Such a distinction of percept from mental image as
being not only externally dependent but also of the moment is probably merely academic, since going behind the
first screen was a percept only a moment before and since
percepts are inherently and immediately a part of already
preexisting cognitive organization. Nevertheless, perhaps
we can find an example in which percept and mental image are not just processed as separate, but in which a percept scheme and mental image scheme of the same object
are merged or confused with one another while the object
is still present. Does the child ever reach for his mental image of an object instead of his percept of it? Does he treat
his mental image scheme as just as real as his percept? In a
manner of speaking, he does.

Prepercept and Premental Image

Before giving examples of this I would like to intro-
duce the terms "prepercept" and "premental image." Pre-

percept refers to the stage-5 child's image that is active when the presence of an object is integral to it, when an external observer might assume the child is perceiving. Premental image is the image scheme that is active when the object's presence is not integral to it. Two different forms of activity of the same basic object scheme could be expected to occur at times, since as early as stage 3 we have seen that not all parts of schemes must be active at one particular time. These two forms, prepercept and premental image, not separate from each other in stage 5, become percept and mental image once the child distinguishes one from the other.

In stage 5 examples of search a child's recent prepercept is processed as indistinct from either a past or present premental image. For example, when Piaget (1954, pp. 72 & 74) enclosed a ring in his hand and then passed his hand behind a screen where he dropped the ring, Jacqueline, after searching his hand, searched his other hand rather than under the screen. When Piaget (1954, p. 75) placed his watch in Jacqueline's slipper and dropped the watch under a screen, Jacqueline searched his vest pocket, not under the screen. The prepercept of seeing-the-watch-disappear-into-the (experimenter's)-hand is not processed as separate from the history, the premental image, a memory of the object's appearing-from- or disappearing-into-the-vest-pocket. But also the scheme of the ring's disappearing-into-one-hand, a prepercept (recent, though past), is not processed as separate from a current construct or premental image, the scheme of its disappearing-into-an-analogous-container, the other hand.

The next two examples show permeability of boundaries between prepercept and premental image schemes which are both current. When Jacqueline was in stage 5, Piaget (1954, p. 201) removed a toy from her rompers through the opening for her thigh rather than through the opening for her neck where it had entered. She had just been looking at the toy. Having the real object in front of her, a prepercept, she nevertheless looked through the neck opening in her rompers where she remembered it had been, a premental image. She acted on her premental image rather than her prepercept. It was as real or more real to her than her prepercept. At twenty-eight months of age, well into the preconceptual or symbolic stage (two to four years), while standing in the garden with her father, Lucienne heard the water running in the house and, apparently thinking of her father washing in the bathroom, declared that he was in the house (Piaget, 1962a, p. 263). She regarded her premental image of his being in the house as just as real as her prepercept of her father who was with her.

In this last instance we have an example of a persisting diffusion of the boundaries between prepercept and premental image occurring after stage 6, in the preconceptual stage. To this author stage 6 and the preconceptual stage are not qualitatively separable. Until after the preconceptual stage, not only are prepercept and premental image separate from each other only some of the time, but also, as has been pointed out, the same limits hold true for separation of object schemes.[2]

In stage 6, in the instance when the child searches behind a second screen for an object, mental image and percept are processed as separate. But throughout stage 4 and apparently even under some circumstances after stage 6, as in the example when the water was running in father's bathroom, an image is best characterized as a percept-mental image combined, a prepercept when dependent on presence of the object, a premental image when presence of the object is not necessarily part of the scheme. In these examples the child cannot quite tell whether he is seeing an object or whether he is imagining it. We get a notion of the quality of a stage-5 child's imagery when we recall that he may touch a ring to the side of a stick, expecting the ring to surround the stick. Piaget (1954) commented that the child does not anticipate impenetrability. I prefer the thesis that the child anticipates penetrability, that his schemes still penetrate each other, much like overlapping transparencies.

Every stage has transition behaviors which' support the likelihood of transition states in development of imagery rather than supporting the concept that imagery is a product of stage-6 reorganization. Toward the close of stage 4, if an object is first hidden and found under screen A, then hidden under B, Lucienne (twelve months) vacillates, searching sometimes under B, sometimes under A, but usually preferring A until at some point when she enters stage 5 and thereafter regularly searches at B (Piaget, 1954, p. 58). Are these competing images? In stage 5 when Jacqueline (eleven months) searches where the object last disappears, screen B, having difficulty raising screen B, she touches screen A. Are these competing images? Sometimes, as late as nineteen months, Jacqueline searches at A before searching B (Piaget, 1954, p. 75). Late in stage 5, Jacqueline searches under a second screen, but not dependably (Piaget, 1954,p. 72). In stage 6, during a series of searches, she occasionally touches the screen under which she last found the object before looking beneath the last screen under which the experimenter's fist passes. These behaviors fit a concept that imagery is present all along as the child, over time, works out which images serve him best.

We may now reconsider Freud's (1953) 1911 concept that mental images form out of hallucinations. Freud proposed that the newborn, when hungry, gratifies himself by hallucinating a percept of the breast. Over the next few months, because he gets milk coincident with the percept of the breast and not coincident with the hallucination, he distinguishes his percept of the breast as more gratifying than his hallucination. Once he distinguishes percept from hallucination, the hallucination is a mental image or thought. Piaget (1954) objected to Freud's formulation, in part because it granted the child preformed ability to perceive, to have a memory of the breast to hallucinate. Piaget (1977), while stating that understanding hallucinations was necessary for a complete understanding of imagery, did not comment on them. He believed the relationship between the genesis of imagery and its disintegration was as yet not understood. He did not include a hallucinatory phase in normal development as suggested by Freud. The imagined object scheme of stage 5, the premental image, is certainly hallucinationlike. It is an image scheme of an object which is active without drawing upon the presence of the object and which is not understood to be separate from the real thing, the prepercept. This hallucinationlike image becomes a mental image when it becomes distinct from prepercept. The prepercept at this same moment, by virtue of the same process, becomes a percept. So at once both mental image and percept are differentiated one from the other.

In this theoretical construct I agree with Piaget (1954) that Freud (1958) erred in taking percept as a given, but suggest that Freud was correct in his proposition that hallucination is both a normal developmental phenomenon and the anlage of mental image or thought. Additionally, here the construction of percept is dated to one stage later than Piaget's (1954) dating, and mental image formation is dated to a much later time than Freud proposed.

While consciousness is not a result of restructuring, self-consciousness is. Self-consciousness is emergent from the complexity resulting from the developing relationships of the central nervous system as it matures and as it consciously and unconsciously interacts with the environment. The position I take is in keeping with Piaget's findings and consonant with his constructivist stance, but at variance with his proposal that the primary mechanism for construction of mental image is interiorized imitation. I suggest that interiorized imitation is only one psychologic mechanism employed by the child in his differentiating percepts from mental images. More fundamentally, I am at variance with Piaget in his proposal of a discontinuity in conscious mental image or symbol formation, its being a product of stage 6 of the sensorimotor period. I assume that consciousness is a given, i.e., wakefulness, which in steps becomes structured and sensed or understood over time as the child structures and understands attributes of self and external objects.

NOTES

1. The word "whole" should not be taken literally, because, as will be discussed in chapter 8, an object scheme is seldom absolutely whole when it is constructed or reconstructed.

2. This state of premental image and prepercept, this undifferentiation of mental image from percept, is not the same as undifferentiation of self from object (i.e., subjective from objective) or undifferentiation of one object from another. Differentiation of mental image from percept of mother, for instance, is achieved when a distinction is made between the picture of mother, present or not, in which presence is not integral to the picture, and the picture of mother in which her presence is integral to the picture. Piaget (1963, p. 327) was cognizant of the undifferentiation of mental image from percept as he commented that in stage 5 "representation is not yet freed from presentation," but this did not have the significance in theory for him as it does here.

Chapter 7

AFFECT

Chapters 2 through 6 outlined how neurological maturation may support cognitive development and how mental imagery and perception are differentiated as waking
schemes. In this chapter the role of affect is addressed.
The psychodynamic and structural approaches of psychologic function are contrasted. Piaget's conceptualization of
the relationships of affect to cognition and his description
of the infant's affects are presented. Then an argument is
made for built-in primary, probably neurotransmitter-
related affects which monitor schemes and feed back into
them, ultimately serving survival.

Theoretical Positions

Affect is the core of Freud's system and is only peripheral to Piaget's body of work. While Piaget emphasized the
cognitive, perhaps to the neglect of the affective, other
cognitivists take a position of extreme neglect. Zajonc

(1980) pointed out that none of the standard texts on cognitive psychology which he reviewed contained in their indices the words *affect, attitude, emotion, feeling,* or *sentiment.* The work of Schachter and Singer (1962), in which subjects injected with epinephrine interpreted their emotions in accord with their situation rather than as a function of the chemical injected, has been a support for this extreme stand. As will be seen, Piaget's position on cognition and affect, like his position on the nature-nurture controversy, is the middle ground.

The following vignettes illustrate that such theoretical positions are not merely academic. Two staff psychiatrists agreed that the superintendent of their hospital repeatedly caused conflict between the adult and children's services or between the in-patient and out-patient services. He would then be asked by his service chiefs to mediate the conflict that he had caused.

The first psychiatrist theorized that the superintendent caused these conflicts in order to experience the sense of power when he settled the conflict. The first psychiatrist offered an affect-based, psychodynamic explanation. In psychodynamic conceptualizations, the assumption is that if someone does something, he wanted to do it and very often if something happened to him, he wanted it to happen to him. If the superintendent ended up being powerful, he wanted to be powerful. In psychodynamic theory affect or energy or motivation drives and directs the system. All is in keeping with psychic determinism. Ultimately, whatever happens is derivative of a wish.

The second psychiatrist offered a structural explanation. To him a repetitive pattern suggested a type of structure. Structure, once built, is not just beholden to affect, but tends to repeat itself on its own. The structure is visited upon varied circumstances. One sees and one does what one knows. The second psychiatrist pointed out that the superintendent caused conflicts between services years ago, when he was only a service chief himself. He repeatedly stimulated the members of his service to revolt against another service or against the former superintendent. If one were to take a psychodynamic stance one might conclude that he likes to cause trouble and to be powerful. An alternate formulation is that, although the superintendent caused repeated conflict, his causing conflict was basically unintentional, that when the superintendent saw and addressed a current issue, he did not connect that issue with other parallel or even identical ones.

For example, sometimes he asked a service chief what to do about a particular problem that had arisen. The service chief studied the problem and sent the superintendent a report containing certain recommendations. A few months later that same service chief was dismayed when he overheard the superintendent request another staff member to solve the same problem. It was as if the superintendent had never received the recommendation. The second psychiatrist proposed that when confronted with a problem, the superintendent wants the problem to go away. He is not interested in a recommendation. It is much like the patient who says, "Why do I get so frightened?" Most often that patient merely means, "I wish it would go away." Also, the superintendent in a sense forgets that a service chief has no power to implement a solution. Of course the superintendent is not truly forgetful. Rather, when he thinks of one service, the other service is out of focus. While the problem is in focus, the lack of power of the service chief is not; while the problem is once again in focus, the previous episode and request for a solution are not; or when one service chief is in focus, the other is not. In this interpretation, the superintendent is what we described in our earlier work (Malerstein & Ahern, 1982) as a symbolic character, a particle-to-particle thinker in the social domain. The second psychiatrist suggested that although the superintendent caused a great deal of trouble, this was not his intent. He certainly enjoyed power, just as he enjoyed his bringing about the elimination of conflict. However, this was not a goal he set out to achieve, but an effect of his style of information processing, a quality of his type of repeating structure.

A case described in our previous book (Malerstein & Ahern, 1982) provides another example of a structuralist interpretation. We recounted the habitual lateness of Mrs. R. While we took into account some of the structuralist aspects of her behavior our emphasis was on the affective and motivational aspects. Mrs. R.'s lateness occurred because she planned to fill every minute prior to any appointment. Accordingly, for her to be on time, every intervening event (her exercises being completed, her full morning ablutions carried out, her finding all her garments, the bus passing by at the exact time, the clerk at the drug store being available the very moment Mrs. R. walked in, her making perfect connections with transportation to her doctor's appointment) must fall in place perfectly. Each person, each object, each event had to integrate perfectly with her schedule, based on what she knew she could do in the amount of time she gave herself. When all factors interdigitated perfectly, which was rare, she arrived on time. She felt triumphant. While we took into account some of the structural aspects of her behavior, we emphasized her need for narcissistic gratification, that each of her needs be met, and her dependence on external events, everything going just right, to value her. We could have emphasized the structural or cognitive aspect that, as she set her itinerary, she saw it only from her vantage point. She saw only how long it should take her to get from here to there or how long for her to do this particular activity or another. She failed to take into account other persons and other things with their priorities and contingencies. Having a scheme of social interactions which fails to take into account different persons' points of view is a type of social cognition or structure. This organization will tend to repeat itself, often aside from any gratification and apparently in spite of frequent disappointments.

The Import of Different Theories

Strictly speaking, psychodynamic theory is not without structure, nor structuralist theory without affect, but the weight given to one or the other in the two types of conceptualization is vastly different. Depending on which theory is embraced, even the affect which one regards as primary in a given activity differs. From the first psychiatrist's psychodynamic view, drive for power continually directed the structures, that is, the forming and settling of conflicts between different services. In the second psychiatrist's structuralist view, the superintendent's recurrently seeing events as separate allowed him to be freshly goaded by the problem each time and only to enjoy a sense of power when called in to arbitrate matters. But the seeking of power was not dominant throughout as in the psychodynamic view.

Additionally, the particular structure which is viewed as primary differs, depending on the theoretical view. The structuralist focused on the division between events. Even if the psychodynamicist focused on the division between events as a structural problem, he probably would look for the affect that is defended against by such splitting. Also, pursuit of the historical explanation of the superintendent's behavior would differ depending on which theory is operative. Antecedents to the superintendent's need for power (or need to split) would be sought by a psychodynamicist. The holding of separate views of social events might be seen by the structuralist as not only the superintendent's best way of organizing his early experiences of his social world (Malerstein & Ahern, 1982), but something that works for him. Under most circumstances this type of thought process is not alterable to an appreciable extent by treatment, but the patient may learn to take it into account. If the superintendent were in treatment, it would be useful to help him to correct for this approach a bit when it caused him trouble. Helping Mrs. R. consider that the bus conductor and the hairdresser may have their own contingencies to deal with might help her to interpose a little correction at times in her standard approach. It is apparent that whether one embraces a structural theory or a psychodynamic one is not merely a theoretical issue. The position taken will greatly affect one's treatment of a patient.

In all fairness, psychoanalysis, the granddaddy of psychodynamic theory, is always dealing with structure. Constantly, this content or that content is in focus. The patient is anxious about this content, disgusted by that content. Content necessarily presumes structure. The defense mechanisms are certainly structures, channels that divert this drive and content or that. The personality types, for instance, anal character, are structures. Clearly, there is no impulse, no symptom, no cathexis nor countercathexis without structure in the sense that one is always angry about or in love with someone or something. There is always content and form to conflict as well as the channeling (a structure) via defense mechanisms of its expression in symptoms. But the emphasis in psychoanalysis is on affect, on energy.

The Legacy of Freud

Freud's (1953) classic paper, *Character and Anal Eroticism,* presented the abiding syndrome of orderliness, parsimony, and obstinacy of the obsessive character.[1] The syndrome's genesis was postulated to be in intense anal eroticism during bowel training. In this postulate, affect, the cathexis of smearing and of expulsion of the feces, frustrated by interaction with the environment, is transformed by reaction formation into neatness and retentiveness. In this same paper Freud proposed a general theory of character structure formation. If the transformation of affect is via reaction formation, the libidinal pleasure (in smearing) is discharged through its opposite (the obsessive trait of neatness). If the transformation of affect is via sublimation, the libidinal interest (in smearing) is minimally diverted (expressed in painting). In such a formulation, affect is a driving force, constantly being discharged through expression of the character trait; yet the particular character trait is a kind of structure that clearly gives the form to content, while the defense mechanism, reaction formation or sublimation, provides an edge or dividing line between one kind of content and another, a line between either neatness or painting and anal play.

Psychoanalytic findings provide the makings for a primarily structural system for understanding clinical findings, for example, the cluster of defense mechanisms, the history of a struggle for control between parent and child, including the struggle around bowel training and the obsessive or anal characteristics. Nonetheless, affect is always primary in psychoanalytic theory. The defense structure is more a channel for affect rather than a structure related to other more coherent structures, a primary factor in organized function. Affect or energy invokes the transformation and sustains the neatness. Without its energic cathexis neatness would collapse like a balloon.

Starting with Freud's early theories of neurosis, psychoanalysis has never lost its affective cast. Even in Freud's structural theory, which postulates three structures, the id, the ego, and the superego, the structures are built out of energy or affect. In his theory, the id is a biological given, a cauldron of structureless sexual and aggressive drives, undifferentiated affects. With the pitting of cathexes and countercathexes, charges of energy, as the id interacts with the outside world, there is built up an ego. Even the formation of the superego through identification with the father is a function of castration fears, projected agression. The superego then may vent agression against the self in the form of guilt and in the process repress sexual desires.

It must be remembered that Freud's theoretical matrix was 19th century physics, and that he did not incorporate modern biology and clearly not embryology into his system. Psychoanalysis basically has held to its origins in an economic, energic point of view: psychoanalysts are always looking for an energic cause—assuming psychic determinism. Cure was first thought to be catharsis. Interventions are made when a high level of affect is in the therapeutic field. Even repetition of structure, as in repetition compulsion or as in working through, is not seen as inherent in the structure itself, but as requiring drive, for instance the death instinct in the case of the repetition compulsion, just as little discharges of energy are required to explain the need for and result from working through. Hartmann's concept of primarily or secondarily autonomous, conflict-free ego spheres liberated the ego to some extent from id roots (Hartmann, Kris, & Lowenstein, 1964). But generally speaking, in practice and in theory, the energic point of view prevails throughout the theory and practice of psychoanalysis.

Theory affects treatment, and treatment affects theory. This was certainly the case for psychoanalysis. Small wonder that when one discusses Piaget's work with a psychoanalyst, he may respond, "Where is the affect? What do you do about affect?" These are automatic questions as he addresses the therapeutic situation. The patient did this. Why did he want to do that? What was his motive? Was he anxious? Angry? Did he feel powerful?

Affect in Piaget

So, where is affect in Piaget's system? Piaget's (1962a, 1962b, 1915, 1968, 1973) comments on affect appear in a scattering of articles and in a set of lectures given in 1954 (1981a). In Piaget's reports of his investigations during the last 30 years, he has included little about affect; whereas his very early investigations of development of language (Piaget, 1971), morality (Piaget, 1965), etc., were not so bloodless. In Piaget's three books (*The Origins of Intelligence in Children, The Construction of Reality in the Child,* and *Play, Dreams and Imitation in Childhood*) on the cognitive development of his three children, he offers at least 150 descriptions of affective behavior which the very young child exhibits along with his cognitive activity. Even though Piaget's focus in these three books was not on affect, current investigations offer few improvements in description of the young child's affects and provide little in the way of new insights into the meaning of particular affective expressions.

Later I will suggest that the minimal emotional endowment of the very young child includes three pairs of affects, which may go awry, but which generally operate as signals to the organism and to the outside world. These three pairs, at the outset, signal pleasure-unpleasure, familiarity-unfamiliarity, and success-failure. To me these are anlagen of feelings of love-hate, feelings of security-danger, and feelings of triumph-depression.

These affects are evidenced in Piaget's (1954, 1962a, 1963) study of his children's cognitive development. He described wired-in pleasure-unpleasure in terms of not-hungry or hungry, crying or not crying, but without specifying the presence of an emotional polarity of pleasure-unpleasure in the newborn. He described Laurent (one month) sucking his thumb in the same manner as he nursed, with "greed and passion (panting, etc.)" (1963, p.

51). At the same age, Laurent was not completely satisfied after eating and sucked his thumb until at one point he relinquished his thumb and appeared "content and satisfied" (Piaget, 1963, p. 53). Piaget (p. 38) recounted that during the first month the child's "calm increasingly succeeds a storm of crying and weeping" as soon as he is in the nursing position. Piaget (p. 52) noted the one-month-old's "anger" at losing the thumb he was sucking. Piaget (p. 78) reported that at about one and one-half months of age the child who cried at feeding time or when interrupted at feeding, ceased crying when he was picked up. Crying resumed when he was set down. This suggests that at this early age "rage" is connected with "expectation and disappointment," (p. 78), i.e., frustration, and is no longer simply an expression of hunger or other discomfort.

Piaget (1963) observed that the first smile appeared at about five or six weeks of age in response to familiar voices and/or faces. This is a bit earlier than reported by Spitz (1965). Piaget (1963) argued that the smile was a response to the familiar. Although the child first smiled in response to human faces and/or sounds, he also smiled at familiar things. I am inclined to dismiss Piaget's later (1981a) remark suggesting that the first smile could be elicited just by movement of an object since he (Piaget, 1963) argued convincingly for the initial smile's bond to familiarity. Fraiberg (1968) and Freedman (1974) reported that blind babies smile as early as normals. This finding undermined Spitz's (1965) contention that the face is a specific releasor for the smile.

It is not clear if strangeness is signaled after the familiar has had a chance to be established or if strangeness and familiarity are differentiated simultaneously. Piaget (1954, p. 5; 1963, p. 80) noted that beginning at five or six weeks a child appeared astonished or worried by unfamiliar sounds and images and smiled at familiar voices or faces. At three months of age Laurent showed "astonishment and even anxiety" in the presence of a new object he would like to grasp, and smiled as he grasped familiar ones (Piaget, 1963, p. 73). At about the same age, he showed some apprehension and timidity when confronted with a stranger (p. 72). Interestingly enough, the stranger might be Piaget himself, when he was not groomed, or an adult neighbor. When Laurent looked at a neighbor's preteen-age son, who resembled Laurent's sisters, he smiled. These instances of apprehension are somewhat earlier than stranger anxiety reported by Spitz (1965) and Bowlby (1969). The important point is that the smile appears to signal familiarity, while anxiety appears to signal strangeness, strangeness presumably being some unusual aspect of a usual scheme.

After Lucienne learned to make objects suspended from the top of her cot swing, from four to eight months, whenever she indulged in this it was "with great joy and power" (Piaget, 1962a, p. 92). This appears to be a sense of success or potency: her scheme worked. Piaget (1962a, p. 7) reported a four-day-old's whimpering. Was this sadness or depression? At about eight months, when Laurent was about to reach for a watch, Paiget (1954, p. 40) covered the watch with a pillow; Laurent stopped reaching and whimpered. At the same age, Jacqueline, unable to retrieve her toy once it slipped or was placed behind a fold in a sheet, looked at the fold, turned over and sucked her thumb or whimpered (Piaget, 1954, p. 37). These appear to be instances of responses to failure.

Piaget made no extended formal written presentation of his views on affect nor did he investigate affect in the kind of detail or with the same coherence that he investigated cognition. This does not mean that he did not consider affect's role in mental processes. It only means that he did not launch the kind of strategic assault on affect that he did on cognition. The most comprehensive view of Piaget's ideas on affect was presented in a course at the

Sorbonne in 1954. Piaget's notes have been edited and translated by Brown and Kaegi (1981). In these lectures he presents a misleading simile when he refers to affect's being an energy source like the fuel making an automobile engine go. Otherwise, from the rest of the text, it is clear that when he refers to affect as the energetics of the cognitive structures, he means rather that affect is a control mechanism, that it regulates, switches activity on or off in the structures.

Among the early elementary affects Piaget (1981a) lists joys, sorrows, pleasantness, unpleasantness, pleasure, and pain. He implies that in stage 1 these affects are biologically given, since in the next phase of affective development, sensorimotor stages 2 and 3, he says that, based on experience, these affects become attached to perceptions. He cautions against assuming that all early affects are biologic givens, stressing that it is difficult to explain the pleasure at being the cause without presupposing cognitive structures. He emphasizes the omnipresence, indissociability, and heterogeneity of affect and cognition at all levels of development. The affective aspect of assimilation is interest while the affective aspect of accommodation is interest in what is new. Even falling in love has a cognitive component, while thinking about theoretical mathematics may include hope for colleague approval. Yet, cognition does not cause affect, nor affect cause cognition as they develop hand in hand. If a stage-3 child reaches for a distant object, the perceived distance is not the cause of the desire. The distance, an obstacle to the satisfaction of needs, leads simultaneously to an intellectual differentiation (some notion of distance) and an affective differentiation (unsatisfied desire). Piaget proposes a continual dialectic between affect and intelligence. The negative affects, sadness, anguish, and anxiety, make their appearance in stage 3 and are joined by the feelings of success and failure in stages 4 to 6. All of these early affects continue thereafter as what he calls the system of regulation of forces constituted by the feelings.

Feelings and Values

Roughly, these feelings correspond to the emotions described by Ekman (1984), discussed below, or what I prefer to call signal affects.[2] In.addition to this system of feelings, Piaget (1981a) described a system of values start-ing to develop in stage 4 when separation of means and end, self and object, one object and another are just begin-ning. *Piaget (1981a) proposed that interest (or motivation) is the coordination of these two systems, the system of elementary regula-tions or feelings with the system of values.*

In his tracing of value development he contended that the form taken for values is always isomorphic to the form taken for development of cognition. Prior to stage 4, there can be no valuing of one activity relative to another since all ongoing activity is part of all other ongoing activity (if it is connected at all). With the beginning of means-end ac-tivity in stage 4, one ongoing activity has begun to be sepa-rate from another, both temporally and affectively. The pillow is struck before the watch is grasped. The watch is preferred to the pillow. There is differential valuation of one spectacle (preobject, preself) over another. In this in-stance the striking-the-pillow has a somewhat negative value and grasping-the-watch a positive one. In stage 5, when a child is able to use the pillow to pull the watch to him, if the watch is resting on the pillow, then the pillow is valued in reference to (as part of) the watch.

Piaget (1981a) traced the development of the value system during the latter half of the sensorimotor period, beginning with the valuation of one object scheme over another, as above. Included are self scheme valuation, for instance, self-confidence, and affection toward other persons, as these object schemes are differentiated. As schemes continue their differentiation from one another on the basis of various parameters, depending on differential experiences resulting in success, fright, and so on they are differentially enriched with affect. Piaget suggested that interaction with persons as opposed to interaction with things has a particularly important role in the development of affect-laden schemes, though basically the difference between valuation of a person scheme and valuation of a thing scheme is only one of degree.

In charting the development of the system of values in the preoperational and operational periods, Piaget (1981a) proposed the same sequence which he had proposed in his earlier work on moral development of the child (Piaget, 1965a), with the child initially, prior to age seven, having a heteronomous superego which corresponds to preoperational thing cognition. For example, in heteronomous moral judgment, one is guilty if caught, as in the intuitive stage a child believes that the car which finishes first is the fastest car. Judgment is based on the end stage, on appearance, that is, on whatever is in focus at the moment. Piaget (1981a) proposed that the eight-year-old's comprehension of his peers' sets of values and vice versa provide the impetus for his construction of autonomous moral values (an autonomous superego) just as he proposed that an eight-year-old's interaction with the thing world yields the concrete operational period in which he is able to classify and seriate attributes of things. A concrete operational child who has 6 daisies and 2 primroses understands that he has more flowers than daisies, though when he was six or seven, focused on the most striking parameter, the larger number (daisies), he insisted he had more daisies than flowers. In parallel fashion, according to Piaget, an eight-year-old is likely to have an autonomous superego. He is able to classify goodnesses and badnesses. No longer thinking that when accused one has done wrong as he thought when he was seven, at eight he insists that a lie includes intent along with inaccuracy, but does not necessarily include detection. Piaget postulated that in adolescence values are ideals embracing concepts such as patriotism at a time when in the cognitive sphere one may embrace the hypothetic, the possible.

Transference

Before presenting my disagreements with his formulations for superego development, I summarize Piaget's (1981a) discussion of transference. Piaget does not doubt Freud's concept of transference, that the child's relationship with the significant figures of the past, usually mother or father, has abiding influence in his later life. For example, when an adult encounters a professor or a psychotherapist, he will react to that person, insofar as he or she represents to him, for example, an authority figure or a love object, as a function of these aspects of his relationship to the caregivers from his early life. With minimal justification, he may tend to submit or to revolt, to adore or to dislike the professor or psychotherapist. Piaget agreed with the interpretation that one's life is dominated by unsatisfied needs of infancy, for instance, a wish for love or freedom. Not entirely resolved old conflicts which remain unconscious may influence and even dominate new situations to the point that behavior in the new situation may be incomprehensible without knowledge of the past. Such an interpretation is the essence of Freud's concept of transference.

The issue for Piaget (1981a) was how these transference tendencies are stored. Piaget viewed transference phenomena not as a complex residing as a whole in the bowels of the psyche, only to escape in full force as a transference neurosis during psychoanalysis, or to intrude and distort current innocent interactions, but as reconstructed phenomena. If one is angry at a particular person about something, does a recording of that person and event plus the charge of affect all reside in some (unconscious) file to be retrieved when one sees that person again, or a similar person? Effectively, this would be Freud's model for conservation of transference phenomena. Piaget suggests that just as one reconstructs an object as one remembers or perceives it, so with a person, so with the event involving that person, so with the affects as parameters of that person (or a similar one), and also so with the affects of the type of event that is part of that person. For example, if one were slighted by someone and had become angry, then in the course of reconstructing that person or a similar one, included in a selection of subschemes employed in the reconstruction would be the event of being slighted. The emotion of anger would then follow once again. So Piaget provides a significant corrective to the theory formulated by clinical observation. In Piaget's view what are conserved are reaction schemes which, like any schemes, have their tendency to assimilate, hence to repeat and to generalize, to transfer. That we react in a similar manner to similar situations is our character[3] and our character is a group of our schemes of reaction.

Superego Development

In regard to superego development, we have disagreed with Piaget on two counts (Malerstein & Ahern, 1982). First, we disagreed that interacting with peers is the usual stimulus for construction of an autonomous superego. We proposed that it is the child's experience with a particular type of caregiver, one who has his best interests at heart, which provides the aliment out of which he may construct an autonomous superego. He learns that his social world, his caregivers, act in accordance with their verbalized rules and, on balance (in spite of momentary discomforts or momentary appearances) behave in accordance with a consistent system with ultimate payoff for him. In their interaction with him a system is demonstrated which works well for him in the long run. He is what we called an operational character. Second, we asserted that, depending upon the type of caregiving experienced by a child, the type of social world of which he is a part, a normal developmental option in our intuitive character is to keep a basically heteronomous superego, or in our symbolic character, is to keep a superego which has a preconceptual cast. It is not necessarily normal or average to construct an autonomous superego.[4]

Brown and Weiss (1982), particularly interested in the function of intelligence as an expression of evolution, bring Piaget's work together with Pugh's (1977). Pugh pointed out that with the advent of high speed computers, the students of artificial intelligence expected that they could solve complex problems, such as those inherent in playing chess, by precisely calculating all possible alternatives to all possible events. When such an approach was attempted with chess, however, after the first few moves, even our largest, fastest computers begin to take endless time to calculate the next best move. It was found that it worked better if one defined powerful configurations on the chess board and aimed toward these. Then playing a good, but not perfect, game of chess within a reasonable period of time became possible. Such an approach is similar to the use of the point system in playing contract bridge. It does not guarantee a win, but it helps one to select a fairly workable contract which then gives one a good chance of winning. Drawing on this type of experience with artificial intelligence, Pugh (1977) suggested that emotions operate as selectors that make success (survival and procreation) probable.

Certainly Piaget's concept of interest, a yield of elementary regulations of forces (emotions) interacting with values, could operate as a selector and thus readily accommodate Pugh's model. It should be understood that in such a system, you do not necessarily win, you do not get perfection or truth. You get something that tends to work, given the parameters of the social and physical world.

Pugh's (1977) list of negative innate emotions is: discomfort, pain, bad taste, bad smell, sorrow, shame, fear, anger, hunger, thirst, and itch. His positive innate ones are: comfort, tactile pleasure, good taste, good smell, joy, and pride. He also assumed that a number of emotions could be acquired.

The fact that members of divergent cultures, sophisticated or isolated and primitive, are able to recognize pictures of facial expressions as indicating particular emotions implies that these affects and their expression are biological givens. Ekman (1984) found that pictures of facial expressions of fear, anger, disgust, distress (probably related to sadness), and happiness were universally recognized. The findings for surprise were weaker; and for interest, contempt, and shame, weaker still. Ekman found further evidence of certain emotions being distinct and biologically-connected when he discovered that either an imitation of the facial configuration for an emotion or an acting of an emotion (à la Stanislavsky) produced distinct autonomic nervous system changes depending on the emotion represented. For example, imitating the facial expression of fear resulted in high heart rate and low skin temperature, while imitating the facial expression of anger correlated with increased heart rate and increased skin temperature.

A Biological Basis

These findings argue for a biological basis for certain emotions and for their facial expression. They do not preclude other emotions also being biological givens, perhaps either not expressed or disguised in their expression in certain cultures. They also do not indicate when these emotions are first put into operation or when they are connected to their facial configuration. Without the connection to the facial configuration and without some clearly identifiable situation, it is very difficult to know when or what kind of an emotion is operating. A six-month-old's response to a stranger versus his mother is sufficiently delineated in regard to situation and his expression is basically analogous to the expression of fear of an older child or an adult so that it is reasonable to infer that fear is being felt by the child. In somewhat younger children, identification of emotions becomes more difficult, as in the smiling at the familiar and astonishment at the new, when the correlates are less easily defined. The fussiness correlating with time since last feeding is probably anger (Emde, 1984), but it could be fear, sadness, or a combination of all three. Similarly, we cannot be sure that the flailing and cry in the newborn evoked by head restraint (Sroufe, 1984) is anger or the forerunner of anger, although it is not incompatible with such an interpretation. Even more difficult to interpret is the whimper of the newborn, though generally we think of a whimper as belonging to a feeling of sadness or depression. Postural indicators of emotions are more difficult to work with than facial indicators (Ekman, 1984). Yet, the prideful or depressed stance could be prewired parts of emotions. Newborns, especially if they are premature, exhibit smiles and frowns during rapid eye movement (REM) sleep (Emde, 1984). REM sleep is generally associated with dreaming. What do these behaviors indicate? With such a sign not coincident with a situation which we can interpret we are in the dark. We may note that the smile/frown are part of the biological endowment, and presume they are part of a pleasant/unpleasant tone, since there appears to be a (negative) correlation with later waking behavior. The REM smile tends to decrease in frequency over the first two months, about the time that the child manifests a waking social smile. REM frowning gives over to nonhunger, endogenous fussiness by two months (Emde, 1984).

Perhaps when our knowledge of brain neurotransmitters is greater, we will be able to trace the development of affects. When we understand the operations of certain neurotransmitters, including their behavioral and subjective expression, we may have a marker for affect.

Psychopharmacological Clues

Recent breakthroughs in psychopharmacology support the position that some neurotransmitters have an intimate relationship to emotions. We now have effective chemical treatments for anxiety, severe depression, and mania. These drugs affect neurotransmitters, the chemicals that pass from the presynaptic neuron to the postsynaptic neuron across the synaptic cleft, to stimulate or inhibit the discharge of the postsynaptic cell. Particular transmitters are found in greater quantities in certain brain nuclei and are utilized preferentially by the systems of which these nuclei are a part. Even though some neurotransmitter systems promise to be the brain sites for primary emotions, many complications remain. While there are separate systems that generally use one particular neurotransmitter, these separate systems ordinarily do not affect each other. When a drug is introduced through the general circulation, however it may affect several systems at once. For example, when we treat schizophrenia with an agent which blocks dopamine, that agent will act not just on the mesolimbic system, which is somehow implicated in schizophrenia, but also in the nigrostriatal system which is involved in modulating motor movement (is antiparkinsonoid). At the same time, antipsychotic agents' action on the dopamine system causes one to raise the question: Since schizophrenia appears to be a thought disorder, are certain neurotransmitters involved primarily in cognition, not affect? Or is schizophrenia primarily an affective disorder? A new antianxiety agent which acts only on dopamine may complicate what we know about antianxiety agents. It is unclear how the action of this new antianxiety agent fits our understanding of the usual actions of antianxiety agents. The action of the usual antianxiety agents on gamma aminobutyric acid and the recent finding of a chemical which acts on the same system and induces anxiety suggests that this system is a combined anxiety-antianxiety system (Paul & Talland, 1984). The finding of endogenous euphoriants stimulated search for other endogenous chemicals which affect emotions. While finding of such endogenous chemicals and their receptors would probably advance and refine our understandings immeasurably, it must be noted that recently three separate classes of endogenous euphoriants (plus many metabolites) have been isolated. So even this neurotransmitter system is quite complex. The action of the antidepressants (Sulzer, et al., 1984) is not as simple as once thought, though they appear to act on systems involving monoamines, compounds which are similar to amphetamines, stimulant drugs. Further complicating the picture is the finding that antidepressants and certain antianxiety agents have been effective in treatment of both panic states and depressive states.

This finding led Klein (1984) to suggest that there is only a single regulator for anxiety and depression. Because Klein found that 50 percent of his patients with panic attacks have a history of separation anxiety, he is inclined to accept Bowlby's (1969) concept of an evolutionarily built-in affect system that protects the helpless infant when separated from the mother, that is, when at risk in the world. This affect system would have a sequence of fear, protest, and depression as described by Bowlby (1969). Such a sequence with corresponding motor activity, such as crying, would serve survival. Initially, cries of protest summon the mother. Failing her arrival, the child gives over to quiet depression, making him less noticeable to a predator.

Profound and relatively selective effects on affect suggest an intimate relationship between certain neurotransmitters and some affects, although many of the complexities of action of these chemical specific systems remain to be understood. At this point we may note how suited some neurotransmitters are to being the seat of basic emotions. Their chemistry and their mechanics, their being relatively confined to certain systems, could play a particularly important role in selecting programs, schemes, that work as they underlie the signal affects which sit midway between the schemes and the need affects (e.g., hunger, sleepiness, need for elimination, etc. which in turn advocate for tissue needs).

Fundamental Emotions

It seems unlikely that the child at the outset feels fully differentiated emotions of sadness, fright, or joy in the same way an adult may; but we would be throwing out good sense to discount the early signs that at least divide pleasant-satisfying emotions from unpleasant-disquieting ones and that very early appear in response to the familiar or strange and to success or failure. In our current state of knowledge and not in conflict with Piaget's observations and theory, we may propose that the young child has three pairs of fundamental emotions, presumably products of evolutionary process. These fundamental emotions have their own positive or negative feeling tone, plus some internal connections allowing them to disrupt (perhaps diffuse) or encourage (perhaps repeat) ongoing scheme activity. Thus they have wired-in connections to the motor apparatus which when activated give rise to certain expressions, for example, smiling. Such motor expressions allow for interaction with the external environment, particularly the mother, who, based on her interpretation of these expressions and on her own agenda, will encourage or disrupt what is going on in the infant, thereby providing external feedback into the schemes.

Initially, deep to the brain's entry points there is little or no division among cognitive, affective, and perceptive activity. To begin with, in the very young child[5], cognition, affect, and perception are each merely activity in certain sets of neurons, while later the distinctiveness of entry ports will be a major parameter in the child's construction of perception and affect as distinct from each other and as distinct from mental images. Activity in certain as yet unspecified brain nuclei or systems will, in time, be felt as rage. That construction of understanding of feelings is not universal is attested to by alexithymics (Taylor, 1984), persons who do not know their feelings. As outlined in chapters 5 and 6, activity in neuronal networks configured as required by the appropriate developmental level will become conscious. But to begin with, any scheme, conscious or unconscious, is part of any other simultaneously active scheme (see Chapter 5). Any activity in the central nervous system is part of any other. The activity in an emotive system and its connections to the rest of the nervous system, including activity at the sensory entry ports as well as activity in the more centrally located neural networks, configurations that have a historical mark, namely, the cognitive schemes, are all to some extent connected to and part of each other. It is likely that this widespread, potential connectedness is actuated to a considerable degree during the first three sensorimotor stages.

Of course, some of the connections of an emotive system and its differentiation from other emotive systems are preformed (or innate), just as some of the connections within the visual system are preformed and differentiated from those of the auditory system. By defining some of an emotive system's interactions with other subsystems, any prewiring determines to some extent that emotive system's relation to the outside world and its impact on the rest of the psychic apparatus. Thus prewiring may significantly determine the construct of the conscious feeling part of this system's activity, especially its distinctions from other feelings. This is consonant with the studies which find a hereditary factor in affective disorders.

Returning to the three pairs of fundamental emotions, I do not wish to suggest that no other emotions or signal affects could be biologically given, but that just three pairs of emotions could suffice, the rest being an amalgamation of one affect with another, or a combination of affect with cognition. I think of these fundamental emotions as distinct from cognition just as I think of sensations as distinct from cognition, with the emotions signaling the state of the schemes and the sensory system signaling the state of the interface of the organism with the external environment.

Consider the pair of affects pleasantness-unpleasantness. This, like the other two pairs, has a range of intensity, in this case extending from love through liking to disliking and rage. The pleasant-unpleasant affect probably has a wired-in connection to an appearance of quiet contentment at one end of the continuum and to fussiness and cries of rage at the other. This affect is also connected to need states: food intake, elimination, pain, temperature, respiration, sleep, sexual tension and pleasure, and probably freedom of movement. When this affect system is active, presumably the organism experiences some kind of contentment or disquiet.

The second pair of affects has to do with familiarity-unfamiliarity. This pair has built-in connections to the smile and to the appearance of trepidation. What is this familiarity? It must be merely a repetition of schemes that have been active in the past. So there must be some scheme buildup before this affect has much play. This appears to be the case since the smile and the appearance of trepidation do not make their appearance before six weeks of age. There is often an alliance between the familiar and the pleasant, hence an alliance with the need affects as well. The same spectacle (mother) that ministers to the child, giving him pleasure, is familiar. The opposite alliance or association may develop in children who form poor attachments to their mothers. If the tie of the familiar to the pleasant were poor enough, the child would not survive. While the look of trepidation at the unfamiliar is manifest fairly early, not until the cognitive achievement of stage 4 when the child begins to differentiate one object from another may we expect to encounter stranger anxiety.

The third pair of affects is responsive to success or failure of the positively valued (pleasant) scheme. Success carries with it a sense of triumph. In keeping with Bibring's (1953) concept, depression is a fall in self-esteem or a sense of helplessness which arises when there is a recognition of one's goal and concomitantly a recognition of the impossibility of reaching that goal, namely failure. This affect, triumph-depression, indicates whether the positively valued scheme which was active was also successful or whether it failed. Not only is a buildup of schemes a prerequisite for this affect, but also some differentiation of schemes is required. Indeed, it was noted by Piaget (1981a) that signs of success or failure appeared later than the other two affect pairs. Interestingly, pleasantness-unpleasantness deals with ongoing scheme activity, while familiarity-unfamiliarity deals with future activity, and success-failure deals with past activity. In order to deal with the future or the past a prerequisite is a buildup of schemes.

Whether we have one built-in affect regulator as proposed by Klein (1984), three pairs (love-hate, familiarity-anxiety, and potency-depression) or six separate affects, or more, it is difficult not to think in terms of biologically given affects that serve survival and signal the state of the organism to the self and others. These affects and their derivatives exert sustaining and diverting affects on the schemes. In signaling the state of the organism they provide an important link in an internal feedback loop. Generally, activity of a negative affect diverts an ongoing scheme's activity as well as future activity of such a scheme. Positive affects feed back into the active schemes supporting and reinforcing such activity currently and in the future. Also impinging on current and future scheme activity is external feedback which depends on the caregiver's (and, later, society's) interpretation of signal affects and how the caregiver (or society) elects to respond to a smile, or to a show of anxiety.

A Balance in Theory

In classic psychoanalytic theory not only is the ego constructed out of affect, but in understanding behavior the cognitive structures are subordinate to affect, as psychic determinism is embraced in the form of "If he ends up in a powerful position, he must have wanted to be powerful." At the opposite extreme, it has been proposed that affect is dictated by the situation, that the biological component of affect is merely arousal, the quality of the affect experienced being a function of the setting (Schachter & Singer, 1962). Similarly, the social cognitivists following Mischel (1968) asserted that personality does not predict behavior, while the situation does. In such a view the subject becomes a respondent organism with no internal structure. The personologists, fighting back, showed that there is some coherence to persons, that not all persons will do all things, based merely on the circumstances, that interior structure has some say (Bem & Allen, 1974; Bavelas, 1978). So the seesaw in theoretical perspective may have found a balance at this point.

Piaget's structuralist position is compatible with such a balance. Piaget's scheme, its configuration being a function of history (experience) and maturation (wiring), is an active agent, which, once used, has an abiding potential for being active again, is much more likely to be active than for activity to be random. The external situation, that is, perceptions, feeds into certain schemes and not others, again due to historical and maturational connections. Emotions and values do the same for the same reasons. Accordingly, current activity in schemes, including thought, feeling, or behavior, may be responsive primarily to affect, cognition, or perception, and in most instances is responsive to a combination of all three. Yet affects probably play a special role in selecting one scheme or another, acting in the present, but also having made certain selections earlier that have left a legacy of schemes.

That primal affects are biologic givens rather than psychological constructs is difficult to deny in view of recent findings of (anti-)anxiety systems and euphoria systems in the central nervous system, and in view of the response of profound affective states (panics, depressions, or manic states) to chemicals. This certainly does not mean that cognition and structure do not influence affect developmentally and dynamically and vice versa. It only means that certain basic affects have their own biological origins and functions.

NOTES

1. Freud's and Piaget's use of "character" differs from mine. For an explanation of my use of the word see Malerstein and Ahern (1982).

2. I prefer "signal" to emphasize the signalling function of affect and do not mean to imply a low intensity affect.

3. See Footnote 1 in this chapter.

4. Integral to each character structure is a form of social cognition which we will not detail here.

5. and in the major affective disorders.

Chapter 8

CONCLUDING REMARKS

Whether one calls consciousness one's soul, spirit, vital factor, or simply awareness, the essence of being alive and human is consciousness. Recently even the law has taken this fact into account, as death has been redefined as brain death, no longer as heart-death.

Then what is consciousness, this essence of being a live human being? How is it related to the organic stuff of which we are made? Particularly, what is its relationship to the brain? These are the two questions I have addressed in this book. I have provided a mechanistic account of cognition, particularly conscious cognition. In my explication of consciousness I draw primarily on the work of Piaget, but also on that of Freud, Hubel and Weisel, and Lecours and Yakovlev.

Having accounted for consciousness merely as mechanics of waking schemes reorganized in the course of development, we may ask, do lower animals have consciousness? Griffin (1981) examined the many facets of psychological functioning in humans, finding parallels for each facet in lower animals, whether it be problem solving, memory, communication, or the use of tools. Evidence for each may be found in various nonhuman animals, bees, ants, sea otters, birds. Griffin (1981) wrote, "This belief that mental experiences are a unique attribute of a single species is not only unparsimonious, it is conceited. It seems more likely than not that mental experiences . . . are widespread, at least among multicellular animals, but differ greatly in nature and complexity" (p. 170). Certainly if consciousness is merely wakefulness and wakefulness is just a state of enhanced connectedness of the central nervous system to the peripheral nervous system, then any organism may be expected to be conscious, provided it has a division between its central and peripheral nervous system and provided it has a sleep/wake cycle. Only the form taken by consciousness would vary from species to species, just as it does from the child to the adult or to a lesser extent from one individual to another.

Consciousness and the Computer

If consciousness is merely parceling out of a mechanical relationship over time, monitored by success and failure, then perhaps a computer could be conscious? In a sense it could if it had an on-off control of the connectedness of its processing system to its input and output terminals and some ability to build an understanding of that on-off connectedness over time with experience. An evolutionary history of many computer generations, however, might be required. If that were the case, if such computers were then to reconstruct themselves, what probably would be constructed would be some type of life form with a sleep/wake cycle.

The model of consciousness presented here is a cybernetic one with considerable parallel to a computer. Nevertheless, not only is it not likely that a computer will ever be conscious, but also memory in a computer ultimately is a point or several points. Whereas, as will be shown shortly, a memory or engram in the brain is reducible only to probabilistic, historic patterns each time to be reconstructed, never perhaps exactly the same, hence never using exactly the same points in space. So consciousness is not to be found among computers, but is likely present throughout most of the animal kingdom.

The Location of a Scheme

Where is a scheme and where is an engram? While there are great as yet unspecified complexities involved, it appears that a scheme is coordinated activity in neural circuits. Some localization is specifiable. Which particular circuits are involved and hence their particular location and function are partly a result of constraints set by the hard-wired parts of the nervous system. For example, sensory fibers from the leg terminate in the upper part of the contralateral postcentral gyrus of the cerebral hemisphere, while fibers from the mouth terminate in the inferior portion of the contralateral postcentral gyrus. In a parallel fashion, motor fibers originate in the precentral gyrus. Such wired-in systems govern location and hence grossly determine a scheme's interrelationships to one neural network compared to another. As a function of maturation, for instance myelination, additional constraints are brought to bear on the location of neural activity.

It must be realized, however, that any such constraints are very broad ones. If one considers the sensory aspect of looking at an object, that object is somehow (perhaps necessarily) the product of a tremendous number of variously organized sensory neural firings. One's eyes scan an object with a number of rapid movements. The object's moving relative to the observer will vary the pattern of the firings.

The data, before getting deep into the brain, are numerous and variable: made up of firings from proprioceptive neurons serving the head, neck, and eye muscles and from the cells of the retina, organized in some measure by whether the light stimulation is in the form of a line or edge, moving or not, and whether it stimulates the right, left, or both eyes. So, while the locus of activity is narrowed to some extent by hard-wiring, there is tremendous potential diffusion of stimuli entering the brain even though the brain, especially the mature brain, is a highly coordinated ensemble of suborgans.

Added to the hard-wiring constraints are those exerted by experience, monitored by affects which signal success or failure. Consider, however, that there are many ways of successfully looking at an object, that there are many ways of striking that object, and that part of one's past history is also included as part of the scheme; all of which reflect the potential location of cognitive schemes corresponding to looking at an object while striking it. Then just a simple secondary circular reaction scheme is widespread and repeated in many different forms of neural circuitry. At the same time that there is this tremendous redundancy, many shortcuts and abbreviations may be called into play. Which set of motor and sensory activities will occur, whether the object will be struck or pushed by the right hand or the left, how it will be looked at this time, and which part of the child's past sensory, motor, and affective schemes will be evoked, all the components of his current cognitive scheme, are highly variable. Hence the locus of neural activity corresponding to a striking-while-watching scheme, let alone a more complex scheme, is probabilistic. It is predictable only in the aggregate. Of course, the visual cortex and motor cortex are involved. At a more detailed level, however, and especially in deeper regions of the brain (beyond the narrowing caused by gates such as area 17), location and particular circuit pattern is probabilistic and, except for the moment, not point-localizable.[1]

We know from someone's history if he will cock his head to look at an object, and if he uses head movement at all when looking at an object; but we can only estimate whether he will do either of these things at a particular time, hence, which particular schemes, which particular circuits will be active, hence, where. As Piaget (1973) demonstrated, a memory generally is a reconstruction. Such a reconstruction may be expected to utilize different components, hence, different locations. As Lashley (1950) showed, there is no point location of memory, no point location of the engram.

I live in a neighborhood of many cars and few garages. I have parked on the street thousands of times in almost every conceivable location within a four-block radius. I have several patterns I follow when I look for parking, though sometimes these patterns disintegrate on an evening when the search is extended. I usually make no special effort to remember where I parked, wishing to get into the house after the day and assuming I will find the car in the morning. Some mornings I remember precisely where I parked. Occasionally, I am at a complete loss and am left to trace my usual patterns, remembering where I parked only after I find the car. I would like to detail the intermediate states, when I cannot remember where I parked as I leave the front door, but as I start to walk I start to remember. In one instance, my first thought was that I had parked in a very unusual place. Then I immediately remembered that as I parked the car the night before, I commented to myself, "This spot rarely has been vacant" [in my 20 years in the neighborhood]. I could then visualize the spot and the act of parking. Another morning before leaving the house (because I was thinking about this problem), I remembered that the previous night I had backed downhill to park in a tight space between two cars.

The car behind me was parked illegally on the corner. I could visualize the truck in front and the car behind. At first I placed the corner as the corner across the street from my house, but then realized the actual parking place was a similar configuration a block farther. It was only then that I recalled that I had not driven my car. I had driven my daughter's car. Mine, in need of repair, was parked elsewhere. So the car that I had remembered was the one that was put in a particular space and the space itself was relocated. The car was more a means of getting back and forth than it was a particular car. Another morning I was again baffled by the mystery of the parked car. I remembered having to give a message to one of my daughters. This message was not from someone at college, where she had been living. It was from someone here at home. As I recalled who had called out to me and the content of the message, I recalled that the previous night I had met him as I walked home from parking the car. Then I was able to proceed.

Of course these instances only sample what must be a widespread unconscious reconstruction of the car. The point is that the car is constructed each time out of some-what different parts—an unusual parking place, a particular location and configuration in space—or assembled from my daughter's car or from a message to my other daughter. An image or memory of a car is possibly never constructed from the same parts, hence rarely in the same neural circuit location, regardless of whether it is in the same location on the street or not. It perhaps goes without saying that the car that I build is not so much parked on the street as it is parked in my head, built less of steel than it is of my experience with it.

What is meant when we say that this mechanistic system is monitored by success and failure, hence makes decisions that work? Where does it work? Primarily it works inside. It serves an internal economy. It has a high probability of working in terms of the external world, serving survival and procreation, but a greater likelihood of achieving an internal balance.

Where is love in this mechanistic-historical probabilistic system? It is located somewhere in Piaget's concept of interest composed of emotions and values and in his adaptation of Freud's transference phenomena, but in a set of subschemes just adjacent to Browning's *Sonnets from the Portugese*. One may complain that this mechanistic system is stripped of life and meaning or one may be impressed that out of material stuff a song of love may be constructed. Of course, the language of love is more commonly found in sonnets, either for ordinary or for psychotherapeutic communications, than it is in striking or grasping or in the abstractions of values and interest.

The Search of Psychoanalysis

Psychoanalysis, the grandparent of modern psychotherapy, for a considerable period of time conceived that genetic insight, understanding how one's current activity reflects earlier experiences, was curative. In psychoanalysis, especially in the movies, the patient would have a blinding flash of insight and then go on to greater things in life. While this did take place with some patients in some analyses, there were patients in whom such experiences did not occur, in whom such experiences led to no change, or in whom the changes that followed were disastrous for the patient. Different psychoanalysts interpreted these responses to genetic insights differently. Some suggested that genetic insight is good for some patients, ineffectual for others, and injurious to still others. Other therapists proposed that genetic insight was good for everybody, but that the therapist must improve his analytic technique, alter the timing, or analyze the negative transference in order to develop a full-blown transference neurosis. For these latter therapists the theory of therapy remained unchanged. To deal with and understand a patient who did not respond to a single interpretation, the concept of working through was proposed, that the energy cathected to the complex must be discharged over here and over there, that one discharge does not liberate the bound energy sufficiently to allow the patient to move forward. In this instance, theory of therapy is changed, but the overall theory of psychological function as a pitting of cathexes and countercathexes against each other, that is, of the psyche as an energic system, remains unchanged.

That the need for working through or the existence of a repetition compulsion implied a structure was not the lesson that was drawn from these discoveries. Time and again, psychoanalytic treatment discovered structures, the oedipal complex, the anal character, the defenses, and so forth. Sometimes disintegration of structure was witnessed, as when a frank psychosis developed during psychoanalysis (a treatment setting of relative isolation, designed to undermine defenses and promote a regressive transference). In spite of the countless encounters with structure and in spite of the legacy of structures which psychoanalysis left us, these structures were not seen as the essence of psychic function. Almost invariably each discovery was translated into dynamics of libidinal or aggressive energy. We are beholden to the psychoanalysts for the structures they found in spite of, or perhaps because of, wrong theory, much as America was discovered in the search for the riches of India.

Still looking for the hidden passage to the riches of India, psychoanalysts did not seem to see that structures that have a significant probability of repetition could be the basis for a new map which could provide a guide for understanding both consciousness and the organic basis of psychological function. I think a structurally-based theory provides us with an improved map, allowing us to discover the byways of the relationship between brain and conscious and unconscious psychologic function.

Structural vs. Energic Theory

What are some of the consequences of holding to a structural theory in contrast to an energic one? If one views the psyche as groups of coordinated, varied, and redundant structures, one expects more stability, more resistance to change than one would expect from an energic system. As already noted, a structural theory readily fits the need for working through or the phenomenon of repetition compulsion. It is not surprising that one interpretation, one insight, one experience does not usually affect the person appreciably. What is required is repeated reexperiences in varied circumstances. It is not surprising that a piece of genetic insight is often so ineffectual and that if it works at all it must be in the transference with a large affectual charge—lived through in all its richness. It is not surprising that when the patient is embarrassed about a particular thought or piece of behavior which need not cause embarrassment in the therapeutic setting, the therapist must point out the patient's embarrassment over here, then over there, then over here, again and again. It is not surprising that a clarification or interpretation must be worked through. Equally not surprising is it that when one loses a loved one or friend, this situation and that, this thought and that, call that person to mind. The construct of that person must be rewritten again and again to take the change into account, to mourn the loss. We used to enjoy a song together, but we can't any more. We had dinner there, but we won't again.

It is the nature of a scheme that it will repeat, whether in the form of repetition compulsion or in transference phenomena. Not only will the scheme repeat, but it will generalize, take into itself what it can at the level it can. If one takes this idea seriously, then one may have to prepare one's interventions to make them palatable to the particular schemes that a particular person has. Such preparation is the fine art of teaching and treatment and sales. Often recognizing that a particular structure is fixed, or vital but fragile, the therapist may elect to provide the patient with a corrective device, a splint or a tool. One may help him to catch himself at times when his standard approach is not serving him well. This kind of limited effort may be frowned upon by depth psychologists and yet may be very helpful in a given instance, or may be what one must settle for, given the circumstances and the limits or desires of the patient.

This is not meant to imply that there is no optimum approach for a particular patient. However, this optimum approach does not lie with a particular school of treatment or even a particular treatment modality. If one thinks of a symptom or syndrome as a scheme composed of an integration of cognitive, affective, and perceptual (situational or environmental) components, all resting on an organic base, then it is not surprising that environmental changes or somatic treatments, as well as psychological interventions, may influence the system. An intervention at any point in this system may affect the system for better or worse. Fortunately, given the system's tendency to adapt, most often it will select the better.

The unpredictability of the psychologic system may mislead one into thinking that one is dealing with a completely plastic system. The problem of predictability might incline one to embrace an energic theory; with an energic model, there is no theoretical limit to change and not much reason to expect stability. But unpredictability should not fool one into thinking of the system as fluid. Rather, the system has a tremendous repertoire to draw upon, given the internal, external, and historical parameters.

As we noted, the line-edge/movement gating system, a maturational factor, is merely an inductor. As a biological factor it does not take the reins and control cognition, but rather provides a new tool which the cognitive structure may exploit. In truth, however, a maturational factor which reorganizes data transmission, as the line-edge/movement gate does, is not quite as accommodating as we suggested earlier. While a line-edge/movement gate functions only as an inductor, rather than exerting total control, it forces a kind of closure on organizations that came before it. No longer will data which pass through area 17 have the same random nature. Something similar probably happens at other stages. If stage change were just a matter of equilibration of what is successful, one might have a rather fluid system, almost like an energic system. An individual could regress completely if things did not work. But such regression is not generally possible. A maturational factor not only offers an opportunity for the door to open to new function, but it shuts the door to old function.

Prewiring

The prewiring of lines and edges, the fact that we generally have the same area of the cortex allocated to language processing, and the prewiring of basic affects give one pause. These types of prewiring assist adaptation to the world and survival. Is it possible that some cognitive constructs are partially prewired? Was Jung correct in contending that certain archtypes are prewired? One does not need these to explain human function, but one should not automatically dismiss such possibilities. Is the Oedipus complex purely a function of being raised by a mother and father and comparing genitals? Or is it prewired in some way? Is alcoholism or homosexuality just psychogenic patterns or is there a prewired tendency? As yet, we do not know how firmly any potential for certain configurations of understanding or behaviors is built into the system. One would assume much latitude, since nesting and hunting tendencies do not categorically separate women from men. Yet we may not dismiss the possibility of inherited potential in such directions.

We do know that certain structures are tenacious (thank goodness), but not predictable in terms of particulars at any one time. It is not surprising that predictions based on personality traits are only modestly reliable (Bavelas, 1978). The psyche is a fascinatingly adaptable, hence not readily predictable, piece of machinery in a remarkable time and space that took a long time to evolve.

Piaget (1973) wrote, "[Although] many problems remain to be solved . . . it is worth thinking on . . . the formation of a general psychology based simultaneously on the mechanisms discovered by psychoanalysis and on the cognitive operations . . ." (p. 48). I would put it a bit differently. We may now begin forming a general psychology based upon the mechanisms belonging to psychoanalysis or psychodynamic psychotherapy, the findings and some of the theory of Piaget, plus the understandings of organic processes.

In this book I attempted to answer two basic questions: What is consciousness? And how is thinking connected to the brain? If I was successful, in the course of answering these questions, some of the mystery will be removed, but also some of the fright, some of the fright of loss of consciousness, something each of us faces at some point. None of the awe of life is lost, yet some of the dread of death may be lost. A mechanistic view of animals' development of conscious thought processes is truly impressive; no less so than a theistic theory of the origin of life and consciousness.

NOTE

1. What aspect of the scheme will be conscious, what affect will be operative or felt, and what particular behavior will be manifest are not predictable except on a probabilistic basis, though they will be consonant with certain overriding rules such as Piaget's for consciousness, recounted in chapter 4.

REFERENCES

Bavelas, J. B. *Personality: Current theory and research.* Monterey, CA: Brooks/Cole, 1978.

Bem, D. J., & Allen, A. On predicting some of the people some of the time: The search for cross-situational consistencies in behavior. *Psychological Review,* 1974, *82,* 506-520.

Bibring, E. The mechanism of depression. In P. Greenacre (Ed.) *Affective disorders.* New York: International Universities Press, 1953.

Bovet, M. Piaget's theory of cognitive development and individual differences. In B. Inhelder & H. H. Chipman (Eds.) *Piaget and his school: A reader in developmental psychology.* New York: Springer-Verlag, 1976.

Bowlby, J. *Attachment and loss* (Vol. I). New York: Basic Books, 1969.

Brown, J. W. Consciousness and pathology of language. In R. W. Rieber (Ed.) *The neuropathology of language.* New York: Plenum, 1976.

Brown, T. A., & Weiss, L. *Some thoughts on Piaget's theory of affec-*

tivity. Paper presented at the Twelfth Annual International Interdisciplinary Conference on Piagetian Theory and the Helping Professions, University of Southern California, Los Angeles, Jan. 9, 1982.

Coyle, J. T. Introduction to the pharmacology of the synapse, In R. E. Hales & A. J. Frances (Eds.) *Annual Review of the American Psychiatric Association,*1985, *4*, 5-16.

Deutsch, H. Some forms of emotional disturbance and their relationship to schizophrenia. *Psychoanlaytic Quarterly,* 1942, *11*, 301-321.

Ekman, P. Expression and nature of emotion. In K. R. Scherer & P. Ekman (Eds.) *Approaches to emotion.* Hillsdale, N.J.: Lawrence Erlbaum, 1984.

Emde, R. N. Levels of meaning for infant emotion: A biological view. In K. R. Scherer & P. Ekman (Eds.) *Approaches to emotion.* Hillsdale, N.J.: Lawrence Erlbaum, 1984.

Fraiberg, S. Parallel and divergent patterns in blind and sighted infants. *The Psychoanalytic Study of the Child,* 1968, *23*, 264-300.

Freedman, D. G. *Human infancy: An evolutionary perspective.* Hillsdale, N.J.: Lawrence Erlbaum, 1974.

Freud, S. Formulations regarding the two principles of mental functioning. *Collected papers IV.* (J. Riviere, trans.) London: Hogarth Press, 1953a (Originally published, 1911).

Freud, S. Metapsychological supplement to the theory of dreams. *Collected papers IV.* (J. Riviere, trans.) London: Hogarth Press, 1953b (Originally published, 1916).

Gallagher, J. M., & Reid, D. K. *The learning theory of Piaget and Inhelder.* Monterey, CA: Brooks/Cole, 1981.

Griffin, D. R. *The question of animal awareness: An evolutionary continuity of mental experience.* Los Altos, CA: Kaufman, 1981.

Hartmann, H., Kris, E., & Lowenstein, R. M. Papers on psychoanalytic psychology. In G. S. Klein (Ed.) *Psychological Issues, 4* (2), Monograph 14. New York: International Universities Press, 1964.

Hubel, D. H., & Weisel, T. N. Brain mechanisms of vision. *Scientific American,* 1979, *241*, 130-144.

Jacobsen, M. Brain development in relation to language. In E. H. Lenneberg & E. Lenneberg (Eds.) *Foundations of language development: A multi-disciplinary approach* (Vol. I). New York: Academic Press, 1975.

Kandel, E. R. Small systems of neurons. *Scientific American,* 1979, *241,* 60-70.

Kaplan, H. I., Freedman, A. M., & Sadock, B. J. *Comprehensive textbook of psychiatry III.* Baltimore: Williams & Wilkins, 1980.

Klein, D. *Anxiety reconceptualized.* Paper presented at Langley Porter Grand Rounds, Department of Psychiatry, University of California, San Francisco, April 18, 1984.

Klein, M., Shapiro, E., & Kandel, E. R. Synaptic plasticity and the modulation of the Ca^{2+} current. *Journal of Experimental Biology,* 1980, *89,* 117-157.

Kohlberg, L. A. The development of children's orientation toward a moral order: Sequence in the development of moral thought. *Vita Humana,* 1963, *6,* 11-33.

Kohut, H. *The restoration of the self.* New York: International Universities Press, 1977.

Lashley, K. S. In search of the engram. *Symposia of the Society for Experimental Biology* (Great Britain), (Vol. 4). *Psychological mechanisms in animal behavior.* Cambridge, England: University Press, 1950.

Laurendeau, M., & Pinard, A. *The development of space in the child.* New York: International Universities Press, 1970.

Lecours, A. R. Myelogenetic correlates of the development of speech and language. In E. H. Lenneberg & E. Lenneberg (Eds.) *Foundations of language development: A multidisciplinary approach* (Vol. I). New York: Academic, 1975.

Louie, A. *Molecular mechanisms of opiate tolerance.* Paper presented at Department of Psychiatry Grand Rounds, University of California, San Francisco, May 2, 1985.

Maier, H. W. *Three theories of child development.* New York: Harper and Row, 1965.

Maratos, O. The origin and development of imitation in the first six months of life. Unpublished doctoral thesis, University of Geneva.

Mason, A. S., & Granacher, R. P. *Clinical handbook of antipsychotic drug therapy.* New York: Brunner Mazel, 1980.

Meltzer, H. Y. Seritonergic function in the affective disorders: The effect of antidepressants and lithium on a 5-hydroxy-tryptophane-induced increase in serum cortisol. *Annals of the New York Academy of Sciences,* 1984, *430,* 115-138.

Mischel, W. *Personality and assessment.* New York: Wiley, 1968.

Paul, S. M., & Talland, J. F. Benzodiazepam receptors: From pharmacology to physiology. *Roche Receptor,* 1984, *1,* 1-3.

Piaget, J. Principal factors determining intellectual evolution from childhood to adult life. In *Factors determining human behavior* (Report of the Harvard Tercentary Conference of Arts and Sciences), Cambridge, Mass.: Harvard University Press, 1937.

Piaget, J. *The construction of reality in the child.* (M. Cook, trans.) New York: Basic Books, 1954a.

Piaget, J. The problem of consciousness in child psychology: Developmental changes in awareness. In *Consciousness, transactions of the 4th conference.* New York: Josiah Macy Jr. Foundation, 1954b.

Piaget, J. *Play, dreams and imitation in childhood.* (C. Gattegno & F. M. Hodgson, trans.) New York: Basic Books, 1962a.

Piaget, J. The relation of affectivity to intelligence in the mental development of the child. *Bulletin of the Menninger Clinic,* 1962b, *26,* 129-137.

Piaget, J. *The origins of intelligence in childhood.* (M. Cook, trans.) New York: Norton, 1963.

Piaget, J. *The moral judgment of the child.* (M. Gabain, trans.) New York: The Free Press, 1965. (Originally published, 1932).

Piaget, J. *Six psychological studies.* (D. Elkind, ed.; A. Tenzer, trans.) New York: Vintage Books, 1968.

Piaget, J. *Biology and knowledge: An essay on the relations between organic regulations and cognitive processes.* Chicago: University of Chicago Press, 1971a.

Piaget, J. *The language and thought of the child.* (M. Gabain, trans.) New York: Meridan Books, 1971b.

Piaget, J. *The child and reality: Problems of genetic psychology.* (A. Rosin, trans.) New York: Grossman, 1973.

Piaget, J. *The grasp of consciousness: Action and concept in the young child.* (S. Wedgewood, trans.) Cambridge, Mass.: Harvard University Press, 1976.

Piaget, J. Mental images. In H. E. Gruber & J. J. Vonèche (Eds.) *The essential Piaget.* New York: Basic Books, 1977.

Piaget, J. *Adaptation and intelligence: Organic selection and phenocopy.* (S. Eames, trans.) Chicago: University of Chicago Press, 1980.

Piaget, J. *Intelligence and affectivity: Their relationship during child development.* (T. A. Brown & C. E. Kaegi, eds. & trans.) Palo Alto Annual Reviews Monographs, 1981a.

Piaget, J. Problems of equilibration. In J. M. Gallagher & D. K. Reid (Eds.) *The learning theory of Piaget and Inhelder.* (E. Duckworth, trans.) Monterey, CA: Brooks/Cole Publishing, 1981b.

Piaget, J., & Inhelder, B. in collaboration with M. Bovet, A. Etienne, F. Frank, E. Schmid, S. Taponier, & T. Vinh-Bang. *Mental imagery in the child: A study of the development of imaginal representation.* (P. A. Chilton, trans.) New York: Basic Books, 1971.

Piaget, J., & Inhelder B., in collaboration with H. Sinclair De Zwart. *Memory and intelligence.* New York: Basic Books, 1973.

Pugh, G. E. *The biological origin of human values.* New York: Basic Books, 1977.

Rapaport, D. Some metapsychological considerations concerning activity and passivity. In M. Gill (Ed.) *Collected papers of David Rapaport.* New York: Basic Books, 1967.

Schachter, S. & Singer, J. E. Cognitive, social and physiological determinants of emotional state. *Psychological Review,* 1962, *69,* 379-399.

Simon, E. J. Recent studies on opiate receptors. *Roche Receptor,* 1984, *1,* 1-3.

Spelke, E. Preferential looking methods as tools for study of cognition in infancy. In G. Gottlieb & Krasnegor (Eds.) *Measurement of vision and audition in infancy.* Norwood, N.J.: Ablex, in press.

Sperry, R. W. Mind-brain interaction: Mentalism, yes; dualism, no. *Moebius,* 1981, *1,* 46-75.

Spitz, R. in collaboration with W. G. Cobliner. *The first year of life.* New York: International Universities Press, 1965.

Sroufe, L. A. The organization of emotional development. In K. R. Scherer & P. Ekman (Eds.) *Approaches to emotion.* Hillsdale, N.J.: Lawrence Erlbaum, 1984.

Sulzer, F., Gillespie, D. D., Mishra, R., & Manier, D. H. Desensitization by antidepressants of central norepinephrine receptor systems coupled to adenylate cyclase. *Annals of the New York Academy of Sciences,* 1984, *430,* 91-101.

Taylor, G. J. Alexithymia: Concept, measurement and implications for treatment. *American Journal of Psychiatry,* 1984, *141,* 725-732.

Vaughn, V. C., & McKay, R. J. *Nelson textbook of pediatrics.* Philadelphia: Saunders, 1975.

Zajonc, R. B. Feeling and thinking: Preferences need no inferences. *American Psychologist,* 1980, *35,* 151-175.

NAME INDEX

Ahern, M., 9, 30, 49, 51, 113-115, 126
Allen, A., 137

Bavelas, J. B., 137, 150
Bem, D. J., 137
Bibring, E., 135
Bovet, M., 30
Bowlby, J., 121, 131
Breuer, J., 18
Brown, J. W., 76
Brown, T. A., 122, 127

Coyle, J. T., 45

Deutsch, H., 17

Eccles, J. C., 73
Ekman, P., 123, 128, 129

Emde, R. N., 129, 130
Erikson, E., 9

Fraiberg, S., 120
Freedman, A. M., 90
Freedman, D. G., 120
Freud, S., 5, 7, 10, 11-14, 16-19, 22, 23, 25-29, 74, 78, 83, 108, 109, 111, 116-118, 125, 126, 137, 139, 145

Gallagher, J. M., 49
Griffin, D. R., 139, 140

Hartmann, H., 14, 118
Hubel, D. H., 51, 53, 63, 139

Inhelder, B., 17, 44, 47, 48, 77, 89

SUBJECT INDEX

Accommodation, 21, 23-24, 35, 46
  and the signifier, 76
Action on, 20, 42, 62, 87
Adaptation, 21, 44, 78
Aliment, 21-22, 23-24, 35, 44, 88,
  93, 98
  See also Assimilation, of coinci-
    dental aliment
Anxiety, stranger (separation),
  120-121, 129, 131, 135
Area, 17, 51-59, 142, 149
Assimilation, 20-21, 23-24, 80
  and the signified, 76
  of coincidental aliment, 86-87
Attribute, 24, 26, 27, 28, 33-34, 98
Automatic function, 25, 68

Boundaries (*see* Edges or boundaries)

Casuality, 37, 70, 72, 73
Character, 113, 127, 137
  structure, 9, 10, 138
Classification, 26, 27-28, 34, 77
Conflict, 20, 68, 69, 112-113
Constructivism, 63
  components of construction,
    80-82
  starting with undifferentiated
    schemes, 35
  and transference, 125-126
  See also Memory, location of
Coordination, 19, 39, 81, 99, 104

Defense mechanisms, 19, 26, 27,
  116, 117
Differentiation, 33, 38, 39, 40, 41,
  52, 59, 60, 74, 80, 85, 88, 89,
  96, 101-102, 110, 123